Arthur Murphy

The Orphan of China

A Tragedy

Arthur Murphy

The Orphan of China
A Tragedy

ISBN/EAN: 9783744661935

Printed in Europe, USA, Canada, Australia, Japan

Cover: Foto ©Thomas Meinert / pixelio.de

More available books at **www.hansebooks.com**

THE
ORPHAN
OF
CHINA,
A
TRAGEDY,

As it is perform'd at the

THEATRE-ROYAL,

IN

DRURY-LANE.

Nuncia fama ruit, matrifque allabitur aures;
Evolat infelix et fæmineo ululatu
Sciſſa comam, muros amens atque agmina curſu
Prima petit: non illa virum, non illa Pericli
Telorumque memor: cælum dehinc queſtibus implet.
             VIRG.

The THIRD EDITION.

LONDON:

Printed for P. VAILLANT. 1772.

[Price One Shilling and Six-pence.]

TO THE
RIGHT HONOURABLE
JOHN, Earl of BUTE,
GROOM of the STOLE
TO HIS
Royal Highneſs the Prince of WALES.

My Lord,

THE generous concern you were pleaſed to expreſs for the anxieties of a young Author, then wholly unknown to your Lordſhip, and trembling for his firſt attempt towards " the graveſt, moraleſt, and moſt
" pro-

"profitable of all poems," as Milton calls a Tragedy, was the diftinguifhing mark of a mind truly great, and endued with thofe fine feelings which are the ornaments of even greatnefs itfelf. To this your innate partiality for every endeavour in the polite arts I muft afcribe it, that the following fcenes met with an early approbation from your Lordfhip; an approbation that was at once the author's pride, and his ftrongeft affurance of fuccefs.

The Public have indeed very far outgone my moft fanguine hopes, in their reception of this piece: but now, my Lord, *The Orphan* has another fevere trial to go through; he muft adventure into the world, unaffifted by the advantages of reprefentation: he muft enter your Lordfhip's clofet, and there ftand the examination of the moft accurate criticifm. *In Metí defcendat judicis aures.* This cannot but be an alarming circumftance to a writer fully confcious of his own inability; who has not been able entirely to pleafe even his own tafte; who defpairs of fatisfying others of a more exalted relifh in the arts, and therefore craves at your

Lordfhip's

DEDICATION.

Lordship's hands that protection to his industry, which he is aware cannot be granted to his merit.

I have the honour to remain, with the truest respect, and most grateful acknowledgment,

    My Lord,

        Your Lordship's

            Most obliged,

                and most devoted

                    humble servant,

Lincoln's Inn,
April 30, 1759.

                    ARTHUR MURPHY.

PROLOGUE.

By WILLIAM WHITEHEAD, Esq;
POET-LAUREAT.

Spoken by Mr. HOLLAND.

ENOUGH of Greece and Rome. Th' exhausted store
   Of either nation now can charm no more:
Ev'n adventitious helps in vain we try,
Our triumphs languish in the public eye;
And grave processions, musically slow,
Here pass unheeded,—as a Lord Mayor's shew.
   On eagle wings the poet of to-night
Soars for fresh virtues to the source of light,
To China's eastern realms: and boldly bears
Confucius' morals to Britannia's ears.
Accept th' imported boon; as ecchoing Greece
Receiv'd from wand'ring chiefs her golden fleece;
Nor only richer by the spoils become,
But praise th' advent'rous youth, who brings them home.
   One dubious character, we own, he draws,
A patriot zealous in a monarch's cause!
Nice is the task the varying hand to guide,
And teach the blending colours to divide;
Where, rainbow-like, th' encroaching tints invade
Each other's bounds, and mingle light with shade.
   If then, assiduous to obtain his end,
You find too far the subject's zeal extend;
If undistinguish'd loyalty prevails
Where nature shrinks, and strong affection fails,
On China's tenets charge the fond mistake,
And spare his error for his Virtue's sake.
   From nobler motives our allegiance springs,
For Britain knows no Right Divine in Kings;
From freedom's choice that boasted right arose,
And thro' each line from freedom's choice it flows.
Justice, with Mercy join'd, the throne maintains;
And in his People's HEARTS OUR MONARCH reigns.

                                              EPI-

EPILOGUE.

Spoken by Mrs. YATES.

THRO' five long acts I've wore my sighing face,
  Confin'd by critic laws to time and place;
Yet that once done, I ramble as I please,
Cry London Hoy! and whisk o'er land and seas——
—Ladies, excuse my dress—'tis true Chinese.
Thus, quit of husband, death, and tragic strain,
Let us enjoy our dear small talk again.
  How cou'd this bard successful hope to prove?
So many heroes,—and not one in love!
No suitor here to talk of flames that thrill;
To say the civil thing——" Your eyes so kill!"——
No ravisher, to force us——to our will!
You've seen their eastern virtues, patriot passions,
And now for something of their taste and fashions.
O Lord! that's charming——cries my Lady Fidget,
I long to know it——Do the creatures visit?
Dear Mrs. Yates, do, tell us——Well, how is it?
  First, as to beauty——Set your hearts at rest—
They're all broad foreheads, and pigs eyes at best.
And then they lead such strange, such formal lives!—
—A little more at home than English wives:
Lest the poor things shou'd roam, and prove untrue,
They all are crippled in the tiney shoe.
A hopeful scheme to keep a wife from madding!
—We pinch our feet, and yet are ever gadding.
Then they've no cards, no routs, ne'er take their fling,
And pin-money is an unheard-of thing!
Then how d'ye think they write——You'll ne'er divine——
From top to bottom down in one strait line.   [Mimicks.
We ladies, when our flames we cannot smother,
Write letters—from one corner to another.   [Mimicks.
  One mode there is, in which both climes agree;
I scarce can tell——'Mongst friends then let it be——
—The creatures love to cheat as well as we.
  But bless my wits! I've quite forgot the bard——
A civil soul!—By me he sends this card——
" Presents respects—to ev'ry lady here——
" Hopes for the honour——of a single tear."
The critics then will throw their dirt in vain,
One drop from you will wash out ev'ry stain.
Acquaints you——(now the man is past his fright)
He holds his rout,—and here he keeps his night.
Assures you all a welcome kind and hearty,
The ladies shall play crowns—and there's the shilling party.
                [Points to the upper gallery.

Dramatis Personæ.

TIMURKAN, Emperor of the Tartars,	Mr. HAVARD.
OCTAR, a Tartar General,	Mr. BRANSBY.
ZAMTI, a Mandarine,	Mr. GARRICK.
ETAN, educated as his Son,	Mr. MOSSOP.
HAMET, a youthful Captive,	Mr. HOLLAND.
MORAT, a faithful Friend of Zamti,	Mr. BURTON.
MIRVAN, a Chinese in the Tartar's service, secretly a friend of Zamti,	Mr. DAVIES.
ORASMING, } Two conspirators,	Mr. PACKER.
ZIMVENTI, }	Mr. AUSTIN.
MANDANE, Zamti's wife,	Mrs. YATES.

Messenger, Guards, &c.

SCENE, PEKIN, Capital of CHINA.

THE
ORPHAN of CHINA.

ACT I.

Enter MANDANE *and* MIRVAN.

MANDANE.

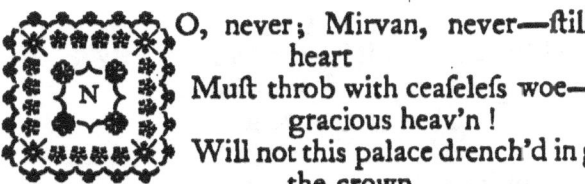
O, never; Mirvan, never—still this heart
Must throb with ceaseless woe—All-gracious heav'n!
Will not this palace drench'd in gore;
the crown
Of China's kings fix'd on the Tartar's brow;
Will not a tract of twenty years in bondage!
Ah! will not these suffice, without fresh cause
Of bitter anguish in Mandane's breast?—

MIRVAN.

Better suppress these unavailing tears,
This fruitless flood of grief.—

MANDANE.

It will not be ——
Ev'n 'midſt the horrors of this diſmal hour,
When fate has all transferr'd from loſt Cathai
To vile barbarian hands;—in ſuch an hour,
This heart, revolting from the public cauſe,
Bleeds from a private ſource; bleeds for the woes
That hang o'er Zamti's houſe ——

MIRVAN.

Alas! Mandane,
Amidſt the gen'ral wreck, who does not feel
The keen domeſtic pang?

MANDANE.

Yes, all.—We all
Muſt feel the kindred-touch;—daily the cries
Of widows, orphans, father, ſon, and brother
In vain are ſent to heav'n;—the waſteful rage
Of theſe barbarians,—theſe accurs'd invaders,—
Burns with increaſing fire;—the thunder ſtill
Rolls o'er our heads, threatening with hideous craſh
To fall at once, and bury us in ruin.

MIRVAN.

And quickly fall it muſt!—the hand of heav'n
Weighs this great empire down. ——

MANDANE.

Nay, tax not heav'n!
Almighty juſtice never bares it's arm
'Gainſt innocence and truth.—'Tis Timurkan,
That fell barbarian—that inſatiate waſter ——
May curſes blaſt the Tartar!—he—'tis he
Has bore down all, and ſtill his ſlaught'ring ſword
In yonder field of death, where Corea's troops
Made their laſt ſtand for liberty and China,
Crimſons the land with blood.—This battle loſt,
Oh! then farewell to all.—But, Mirvan, ſay,
How came the tidings? ——

MIRVAN.

MIRVAN.

From yon lofty tow'r,
As my eyes, straining tow'rd the distant plain,
Sent forth an anxious look, thro' clouds of dust
The savage bands appear'd; the western sun
Gleam'd on their burnish'd helms;—— and soon a
    shout
From the glad multitude proclaim'd th' approach
Of Timurkan; elated with new conquest,
The tyrant comes, and where his wrath will stop
Heav'n only knows.——

MANDANE.

Oh! there—there lies the thought
At which imagination starts, appall'd
With horror at the scene her busy workings
Have colour'd to my sight—there lies the thought
That wakens all a mother's fears—alas!
I tremble for my son ——

MIRVAN.

Your son!—kind heav'n!
Have you not check'd his ardour?—with your tears,
Your soft authority, restrain'd the hero
From the alarms of war?——

MANDANE.

Alas, good Mirvan,
Thou little know'st his danger—but that truth
Must never pass these lips.——

MIRVAN.

I hope Mandane
Doubts not my honest zeal—full well you know
I bear this tyrant deep and mortal hate;
That under him I list, and wear this garb
In hopes that some occasion may arrive,
When I may strike an unexpected blow,
And do my country right.

MANDANE.

MANDANE.

Thy loyalty,
Thy truth, and honour have been ever spotless.
Besides thy wrongs, thy countless wrongs, the wounds
He gave your injur'd family and name,——

MIRVAN.

Alas! those wounds must still lie bleeding here,
Untented by the hand of time—Not all
His lenient arts, his favours heap'd upon me,
Shall cool the burning anguish of my soul.
What he, that slew my father! dragg'd my sister,
Blooming in years, to his detested bed!
Yes, tyrant, yes;—thy unextinguish'd foe
Dwells in this bosom.—Surely then to me
Mandane may reveal her griefs—her wrongs
Will add new fuel to my hidden fires,
And make them burn more fiercely.—

MANDANE.

Urge no more ——
My woes must rest conceal'd—yet should the tyrant
Learn from the captives of yon vanquish'd host,
That China's orphan breathes the vital air,
And to himself unknown, within his breast
Unconscious bears the gen'rous glowing flame
Of all the virtues of his royal line;
Oh! should they know that the dear youth survives,
That for his righteous cause this war began,
Their fury then would kindle to a blaze,
Might wrap the world in flames, and in the ruin
My blameless son must perish.

MIRVAN.

Seek not thus
To multiply the ills that hover round you;
Nor from the stores of busy fancy add
New shafts to fortune's quiver.—Zamti's care
Hath still deceiv'd suspicion's wakeful eye;

And

And o'er the Mandarine his manners pure,
And sacred function have diffused an air
Of venerable awe, which e'en can teach
These northern foes to soften into men.
    MANDANE.
Yes, Mirvan, yes—Religion wears a mien
In Zamti's person so severely mild,
That the fierce Scythian rests upon his spear,
And wonders what he feels.—Such is the charm
Of heart-felt virtue; such is nature's force
That speaks abroad, and in rude northern hearts
Can stamp the image of an awful God.
From that source springs some hope:—Wretch that
  I am!
Hope idly flutters on my trembling tongue,
While melancholy brooding o'er her wrongs,
Lays waste the mind with horror and despair.
—What noise is that?—
    MIRVAN.
Compose this storm of grief;
In ev'ry sound your fancy hears the Tartar——
Your husband this way bends——
    MANDANE.
Celestial pow'rs!
What lab'ring sighs heave in his breast?—— what
  terror
Rolls in the patriot's eye?—haste, Mirvan, hence;
Again look out; gather the flying news,
And let me know each circumstance of ruin.
      [*Exit* Mirvan.

Enter ZAMTI.

    MANDANE.
Zamti!
    ZAMTI.
Mandane!
        MANDANE.

MANDANE.

Ah! what haſt thou ſeen?
What haſt thou heard?—tell me,—has fate decreed
The doom of China!

ZAMTI.

China is no more;——
The eaſtern world is loſt—this mighty empire
Falls with the univerſe beneath the ſtroke
Of ſavage force—falls from it's tow'ring hopes;
For ever, ever fall'n!

MANDANE.

Yet why, ye pow'rs!
Why ſhould a tyrant, train'd to luſt and murder,
A lawleſs ravager from ſavage wilds,
Where chearful day ne'er dawns, but low'ring heav'n
For ever rolls a turbulence of clouds;
Why ſhould a monſter thus uſurp the world,
And trample fair ſimplicity from ill
Beneath his ruffian feet?——

ZAMTI.

Far hence, Mandane,
Thoſe happy days, alas! are fled, when peace
Here nurs'd her blooming olives, and ſhed round
Her foſt'ring influence.—In vain the plan
Of ſacred laws, by hoary elders taught,
Laws founded on the baſe of public weal,
Gave leſſons to the world.—In vain Confucius
Unlock'd his radiant ſtores of moral truth;
In vain bright ſcience, and each tender muſe,
Beam'd ev'ry elegance on poliſh'd life——
Barbarian pow'r prevails. —— Whate'er our ſages taught,
Or genius could inſpire, muſt fade away,
And each fair virtue wither at the blaſt
Of northern domination.

MANDANE.

MANDANE.

Fatal day!
More fatal e'en than that, which first beheld
This race accurs'd within these palace walls,
Since hope, that balm of wretched minds, is now
Irrevocably lost.——

ZAMTI.

Name not the day,
Which saw this city sack'd—fresh stream my eyes,
Fresh bleeds my heart, whene'er the sad idea
Comes o'er my tortur'd mind.—Why, cruel pow'rs!
Why in that moment could not Zamti fall?

MANDANE.

Thy sanctity, the symbol of thy God,
Made ev'n the conqueror suspend his blow,
And murmur soft humanity.——High heav'n
Protected thee for its own great designs;
To save the royal child, the new-born babe,
From the dire slaughter of his ancient line.

ZAMTI.

Yes, my Mandane, in that hour of carnage,
For purposes yet in the womb of time,
I was reserv'd.——I was ordain'd to save
The infant boy; the dear, the precious charge,
The last of all my kings;—full twenty years
I've hid him from the world, and from himself,
And now I swear——Kneel we together here;
While in this dreadful pause our souls renew
Their solemn purpose.——   *Both kneel.*
Thou all-gracious Being,
Whose tutelary care hath watch'd the fate
Of China's Orphan, who hast taught his steps
The paths of safety, still invelop him
In sev'nfold night, till your own hour is come;
Till your slow justice see the dread occasion
To rouse his soul, and bid him walk abroad

B 4   Vicegerent

Vicegerent of your pow'r;—and if thy servant,
Or this his soft associate, e'er defeat
By any word or deed the great design,
Then straight may all your horrible displeasure
Be launch'd upon us from your red right arm,
And in one ruin dash us both together,
The blasted monuments of wrath.——

MANDANE.

That here
Mandane vows ne'er to betray his cause,
Be it enroll'd in the records of heav'n! *Both rise.*

ZAMTI.

And now my heart more lightly beats; methinks
With strength redoubled I can meet the shock
Of adverse fate.

MANDANE.

And lo! the trial comes——
For see where Etan mourns—See where the youth,
Unknowing of the storm that gathers o'er him,
Brings some new tale of woe.——

Enter ETAN.

ETAN.

My honour'd father,
And you, my helpless mother,—ah! where now,
Illustrious wretched pair, where will ye fly?
Where will your miseries now find a shelter?

ZAMTI.

In virtue—I and this dear faithful woman,
We ask no more.——

MANDANE.

Ah! quickly, Etan, say
What means that pallid look?—what new event
Brings on the work of fate?——

ZAMTI.

ZAMTI.
Say, does the tyrant
Return unglutted yet with blood?——

ETAN.
He does;
Ev'n now his triumph moves within the gates
In dread barbaric pomp:—the iron swarms
Of Hyperboreans troop along the streets,
Reeking from slaughter; while, from gazing crowds
Of their dire countrymen, an uproar wild
Of joy ferocious thro' th' astonish'd air
Howls like a northern tempest:—O'er the rest,
Proud in superior eminence of guilt,
The tyrant rides sublime.—Behind his car
The refuse of his sword, a captive train
Display their honest scars, and gnash their teeth
With rage and desperation.——

MANDANE.
Cruel fate!

ETAN.
With these a youth, distinguish'd from the rest,
Proceeds in sullen march.—Heroic fire
Glows in his cheek, and from his ardent eye
Beams amiable horror.——

MANDANE.
What of this youth?

ZAMTI.
Be not alarm'd, Mandane—What of him?

ETAN.
On him all eyes were fix'd with eager gaze,
As if their spirits, struggling to come forth,
Would strain each visual nerve,— while thro' the
    crowd
A busy murmur ran—" If fame say right,
" Beneath that habit lurks a prince; the last

" Of

"Of China's race."—The rumour spreads abroad
From man to man; and all with loud acclaim
Denounce their vengeance on him.——

MANDANE.

Ha! what say'st thou, Etan?
Heav'ns how each black'ning hour in deeper horror
Comes charg'd with woe!

ZAMTI.

It cannot be.—Ye vain,
Ye groundless terrors hence. —— *Aside.*

MANDANE.

My honour'd lord,
Those eyes upturn'd to heav'n, alas! in vain,
Declare your inward conflict.——

ZAMTI.

Lov'd Mandane,
I prithee leave me—but a moment leave me.—
Heed not the workings of a sickly fancy,
Wrought on by every popular report.
Thou know'st with Morat I convey'd the infant
Far as the eastern point of Corea's realm;
There where no human trace is seen, no sound
Assails the ear, save when the foaming surge
Breaks on the shelving beach, that there the youth
Might mock their busy search. — Then check thy
    fears——
Retire, my love, awhile; I'll come anon,—
And fortify thy soul with firm resolve,
Becoming Zamti's wife. ——

MANDANE.

Yes, Zamti's wife
Shall never act unworthy of her lord.
Then hence I'll go, and satisfy each doubt
This youthful captive raises in my heart,

Quick

Quick panting with its fears.—And O ye pow'rs!
Protect my son, my husband, and my king!
                              [*Exit* Mandane.

         ZAMTI *and* ETAN.

              ZAMTI.
Come hither, Etan—thou perceiv'ft the toils
That now incircle me——

              ETAN.
                       Alas! too well
I fee th' impending ftorm.—But furely, fir,
Should this young captive prove the royal Orphan,
You'll never own th' important truth.——

              ZAMTI.
                     Dream not, young man,
To ftand fecure, yet blooming into life,
While vengeance hovers o'er your father's head.
The ftock once fallen, each fcyon muft decay.

              ETAN.
Then let me perifh;—witnefs for me, heav'n,
Could Etan's fall appeafe the tyrant's wrath,
A willing victim he would yield his life,
And afk no greater boon of heav'n.

              ZAMTI.
                     This zeal
So fervid in a ftranger's caufe ——

              ETAN.
                                 A ftranger! he!
My king a ftranger!—Sir, you never meant it—
Perhaps you would explore the fiery feeds
Of Etan's temper, ever prompt to blaze
At honour's facred name.—Perifh the man,
Who, when his country calls him to defend
The rights of human kind, or bravely die,

                                        Who

Who then to glory dead can shrink aghast,
And hold a council with his abject fears.

ZAMTI.

These tow'rings of the soul, alas! are vain.
I know the Tartar well—should I attempt
By any virtuous fraud to veil the truth,
His lion-rage again shall stalk abroad,
Again shall quaff the blood of innocence;
And for Zaphimri all the poor remains
Of China's matrons, and her hoary sires,
Her blooming virgins, and her lisping babes,
Shall yield their throats to the fell murd'rer's knife,
And all be lost for ever——

ETAN.

Then at once
Proclaim him to the world; each honest hand
Will grasp a sword, and, 'midst the circling guards,
Reach the usurper's heart—or should they fail,
Should overwhelming bands obstruct the deed,
They'll greatly dare to die!—better to die
With falling liberty, than basely lead
An ignominious life.—Zaphimri lost,
Ne'er shall fair order dawn, but thro' the land
Slav'ry shall clank her chains, and violation,
Rapine, and murder riot at the will
Of lust and lawless pow'r.

ZAMTI.

Thou brave young man,
Indulge my fond embrace—Thy lovely ardor
It glads me thus to see.—To ease at once
Thy gen'rous fears,—the prince Zaphimri's safe;
Safe in my guardian care——

ETAN.

This pris'ner, sir,
He does not then alarm you?

ZAMTI.

ZAMTI.

No! from thence
I've nought to fear.——

ETAN.

Oh! sir, inform your son
Where is the royal heir?

ZAMTI.

Seek not too soon
To know that truth—now I'll disclose the work,
The work of vengeance, which my lab'ring soul
Has long been fashioning.—Ev'n at this hour
Stupendous ruin hovers o'er the heads
Of this accursed race——

ETAN.

Ruin!

ZAMTI.

I'll tell thee——
When Timurkan led forth his savage bands,
Unpeopling this great city, I then seiz'd
The hour, to tamper with a chosen few,
Who have resolv'd, when the barbarians lie
Buried in sleep and wine, and hotly dream
Their havock o'er again,—then, then, my son,
In one collected blow to burst upon 'em;
Like their own northern clouds, whose midnight horror
Impending o'er the world, at length breaks forth
In the vaunt lightning's blaze, in storms and thunder
Thro' all the red'ning air, till frighted nature
Start from her couch, and waken to a scene
Of uproar and destruction.——

ETAN.

Oh! my father,
The glorious enterprize!

ZAMTI.

ZAMTI.

Mark me, young man.——
Seek thou my friends, Orasming and Zimventi.
In the dim holy cloisters of yon temple
Thou'lt find them musing—near Osmingti's tomb
I charge they all convene; and there do thou
Await my coming.—Bid them ne'er remit
Their high heroic ardor; let them know,
Whate'er shall fall on this old mould'ring clay,
The tyrant never shall subdue my mind.

End of the First ACT.

ACT II.

Enter ZAMTI.

ZAMTI.

REAM on, deluded tyrant; yes, dream on
In blind security:—whene'er high heav'n
Means to destroy, it curses with illusion,
With error of the mind.—Yes, wreak thy fury
Upon this captive youth;—whoe'er he is,
If from his death this groaning empire rise,
Once more itself, resplendent, rich in arts
That humanize the world,—he pays a debt
Due to his King, his Country, and his God.
His father,—wheresoe'er he dwell,—in tears
Shall tell the glory on his boy deriv'd;
And ev'n his mother, 'midst her matron shrieks,
Shall bless the childbed pang that brought him forth
To this great lot, by fate to few allow'd!——
What would'st thou, Mirvan?——

Enter MIRVAN.

MIRVAN.

Eagerly without
A rev'rend stranger craves access to Zamti——
His head hoary with age, with galling tears
His eyes suffus'd; his ev'ry look impatience——

ZAMTI.

Give him admittance—— [*Exit* Mirvan.
—— How my spirits rush
Tumultuous

Tumultuous to my heart—what may this mean?
Lo! where he comes——

Enter MORAT.

MORAT.

Zamti!——

ZAMTI.

Ha!—thro' the veil
Of age, that face—that mien—Morat!

MORAT.

Oh! Zamti!
Let me once more embrace thee——

ZAMTI.

Good old man! *They embrace.*
But wherefore art thou here?—what of my boy?

MORAT.

Ah! what indeed?—Ev'n from the ocean's margin,
Parch'd with the sun, or chill'd with midnight damps,
O'er hills, and rocks, and dreary continents,
In vain I've follow'd——

ZAMTI.

Why didst let him forth?

MORAT.

Think not thy Morat urg'd him to the deed.
His valour was the cause; and soon as fame
Proclaim'd the prince alive, the mighty din
Of preparation thro' all Corea's realm
Alarm'd his breast—Indignant of controul
He burst his covert, and now, hapless youth—

ZAMTI.

Ah!—dead!—in battle fall'n!——

MORAT.

MORAT.

Alas! ev'n now
He drags the conqu'ror's chain.——

ZAMTI.

Mandane then
May still embrace her son.—My boy may live,
To know the sweets of freedom, ere he die.

MORAT.

Alas! the measure of your woes is full.
Unconscious of our frauds, the tyrant thinks
The prince his pris'ner in your son.——

ZAMTI.

Ah!—Morat!

MORAT.

Wild thro' the streets the foe calls out on Zamti.
Thee they pronounce the author of this fraud;
And on your Hamet threaten instant vengeance.

ZAMTI.

There was but this—but this, ye cruel pow'rs,
And this you've heap'd upon me.—Was it not
Enough to tear him from his mother's arms,
Doom'd for his prince to wander o'er the world?
—Alas! what needed more?—Fond foolish eyes
Stop your unbidden gush—tear, tear me piecemeal—
—No, I will not complain—but whence on him
Could that suspicion glance?——

MORAT.

This very morn,
Ere yet the battle join'd, a faithful messenger,
Who thro' the friendly gloom of night had held
His darkling way, and pass'd the Tartar's camp,
Brought me advices from the Corean chief,——
That soon as Hamet join'd the warlike train,
His story he related.—Straight the gallant leader

C   With

With open arms receiv'd him — knew him for thy
    son,
In secret knew him, nor reveal'd he aught
That touch'd his birth.—But still the busy voice
Of fame, increasing as she goes, thro' all the ranks
Babbled abroad each circumstance.—By thee
How he was privately convey'd—sent forth
A tender infant to be rear'd in solitude,
A stranger to himself!—The warriors saw
With what a graceful port he mov'd in arms,
An early hero! deem'd him far above
The common lot of life—deem'd him Zaphimri,
And all with reverential awe beheld him.
This, this, my Zamti, reach'd the tyrant's ear,
And rises into horrid proof.——

              ZAMTI.
If so,
Oh! what a sacrifice must now be made!   *Aside.*

              MORAT.
But when the secret shall be known——

              ZAMTI.
Oh! Morat!
Does thy poor bleeding country still remain
Dear to thy heart?—Say, dost thou still revere
That holy pow'r above, Supreme of beings,
Mistaken by the Bonzée, whom our fathers
Worship'd in happier days!——

              MORAT.
He,—only he
For twenty years hath given me strength in exile.

              ZAMTI.
Then bending here, before his awful throne,
Swear what I now unfold, shall ever lie
In sacred silence wrapp'd——

              MORAT.

MORAT.

I swear!——

ZAMTI.

Now mark me ——
Morat—my son—*(turning aside)* Oh! cruel, cruel
    task,
To conquer nature while the heart-strings break.—

MORAT.

Why heave those sighs?— and why that burst of
    grief?

ZAMTI.

My son—his guiltless blood—I cannot speak——
                                          Bursts into tears.

MORAT.

Ha!—Wilt thou shed his blood?——

ZAMTI.

Thou wretched father!——   *Half aside.*

MORAT.

Oh! had you known the virtues of the youth;
His truth, his courage, his enlighten'd mind——

ZAMTI.

I prithee urge no more—here nature's voice
Speaks in such pleadings:—Such reproaches, Morat,
—Here in my very heart—give woundings here,
Thou can'st not know—and only parents feel—

MORAT.

And wilt thou, cruel in thy tears ——

ZAMTI.

Nay cease,
In pity to a father cease.—Think, Morat,
Think of Zaphimri——

MORAT.

Ah! how fares the prince?

ZAMTI.

ZAMTI.

He fares, my Morat, like a God on earth,
Unknowing his celestial origin:
Yet quick, intense, and bursting into action;
His great heart lab'ring with he knows not what
Prodigious deeds!—Deeds, which ere long shall
rouze,
Astonish, and alarm the world.——

MORAT.

What mean
Those mystic sounds?

ZAMTI.

Revenge, conquest, and freedom!——

MORAT.

Conquest and freedom!

ZAMTI.

Ay!—Conquest and freedom!
The midnight hour shall call a chosen band
Of hidden patriots forth; who, when the foe
Sinks down in drunken revelry, shall pour
The gather'd rage of twenty years upon him,
And vindicate the eastern world.——

MORAT.

By heav'n!
The news revives my soul.——

ZAMTI.

And can'st thou think,
To save one vulgar life, that Zamti now
Will marr the vast design?—No; let him bleed,
Let my boy bleed:—in such a cause as this
I can resign my son—with tears of joy
Resign him,—and one complicated pang
Shall wrench him from my heart.——
The conqu'ror comes! *Warlike music within.*
This

This is no hour for parlying—Morat, hence,
And leave me to my fix'd refolve. ⸺

MORAT.
Yet think,
Think of fome means to fave your Hamet. ⸺

ZAMTI.
Oh!
It cannot be—the foul of Timurkan
Is bold and ftirring—when occafion calls,
He fprings aloft, like an expanding fire,
And marks his way with ruin.—Now he knows
Zaphimri lives, his fear will make him daring
Beyond his former crimes—for joy and riot
Which this day's triumph brings, remorfelefs rage
And maffacre fucceed—and all our hopes
Are blafted, for an unimportant boy.
A fecond Flourifh.

MORAT.
That nearer found proclaims his dread approach—
Yet once more, Zamti, think ⸺

ZAMTI.
No more—I'll fend
Thofe fhall conduct thee where Orafming lives—
There dwell, unfeen of all.—But, Morat, firft
Seek my Mandane.—Heav'ns! how fhall I bear
Her ftrong impetuofity of grief,
When fhe fhall know my fatal purpofe?—Thou
Prepare her tender fpirit; footh her mind,
And fave, oh! fave me from that dreadful conflict.
[Exeunt.

Two large Folding-gates in the Back-scene are burst open by the Tartars, *and then enter* Timurkan, *with his Train.*

TIMURKAN.
Hail to this regal dome, this gorgeous palace!
Where this inventive race have lavish'd all
Their elegance;—ye gay apartments hail!
Beneath your storied roof, where mimick life
Glows to the eye, and at the painter's touch
A new creation lives along the walls;
Once more receive a conqueror, arriv'd
From rougher scenes, where stern rebellion dar'd
Draw forth his phalanx; till this warlike arm
Hurl'd desolation on his falling ranks,
And now the monster, in yon field of death,
Lies overwhelm'd in ruin.—

OCTAR.
There he fell,
No more to stalk thy realm; the eastern world
From this auspicious day, beneath your feet
Lies bound in adamantine chains.———

TIMURKAN.
Thus, Octar,
Shall Timurkan display his conqu'ring banners,
From high Samarcand's walls, to where the Tanais
Devolves his icy tribute to the sea.———

OCTAR.
But first this captive prince.———

TIMURKAN.
Yes, Octar, first
Zaphimri gluts my rage—bring him before us—first
We'll crush the seeds of dark conspiracy—
For Zamti—he, that false insidious slave,
Shall dearly pay his treasons.———

OCTAR.

OCTAR.

Zamti's crimes
'Twere best to leave unpunished :—vers'd in wiles,
Of sly hypocrisy, he wins the love
Of the deluded multitude.—'Twould seem,
Should we inflict that death his frauds deserve,
As if we meant destruction to their faith :
When a whole people's minds are once inflam'd
For their religious rights, their fury burns
With rage more dreadful, as the source is holy.—

TIMURKAN.

Octar, thou reason'st right :—henceforth my art
To make this stubborn race receive the yoke,
Shall be by yielding to their softer manners,
Their vesture, laws, and customs : thus to blend
And make the whole one undistinguish'd people.
The boy comes forth in sullen mood—what passions
Swell in his breast in vain !——

Enter HAMET, *in Chains.*

TIMURKAN.

Thou art the youth,
Who mow'd our battle down, and flesh'd your sword
In many a slaughter'd Tartar. ——

HAMET.

True ;—I am.——

TIMURKAN.

Too well I mark'd thy rage, and saw thee hew
A wasteful passage thro' th' embattled plain.

HAMET.

Then be thou witness for me, in that hour
I never shunn'd your thickest war ;—and if
In yonder field, where my poor countrymen
In mangled heaps lie many a rood extended,
Kind fate had doom'd me to a noble fall,
With this right arm I earn'd it. ——

TIMURKAN.

TIMURKAN.

Say, what motive
Unsheath'd thy rebel blade, and bad thee seek
These wars?—

HAMET.

The love of honourable deeds;
The groans of bleeding China, and the hate
Of tyrants.

TIMURKAN.

Ha!—take heed, rash youth—I see
This lesson has been taught thee.—Octar, haste,
Seek me the Mandarine—let him forthwith
Attend me here. *(Exit* Octar.)—Now tremble at
 my words!
Thy motive to these wars is known—thou art
Zaphimri.——

HAMET.

I Zaphimri!

TIMURKAN.

False one, yes;
Thou art Zaphimri—thou!—whom treach'rous
 guile
Stole from my rage, and sent to distant wilds,
Till years and horrid counsel should mature thee
For war and wild commotion.—

HAMET.

I the prince!
The last of China's race! nay mock not majesty,
Nor with the borrow'd robes of sacred kings
Dress up a wretch like me—were I Zaphimri,
Think'st thou thy trembling eye could bear the shock
Of a much-injur'd king?—could'st thou sustain it?
Say, could'st thou bear to view a royal Orphan,
Whose father, mother, brother, sisters, all
Thy murd'rous arm hath long since laid in dust?
Whose native crown on thy ignoble brow
Thou dar'st dishonour?—whose wide-wasted country
Thy arms have made a wilderness?—

TIMURKAN.

TIMURKAN.

I see
Thou haft been tutor'd in thy lone retreat
By fome fententious pedant.—Soon thefe vain,
Thefe turgid maxims fhall be all fubdued
By thy approaching death.——

HAMET.

Let death come on;
Guilt, guilt alone fhrinks back appall'd—the brave
And honeft ftill defy his dart; the wife
Calmly can eye his frown;—and mifery
Invokes his friendly aid to end her woes.—

TIMURKAN.

Thy woes, prefumptuous youth, with all my fears,
Shall foon lie buried.

Enter ZAMTI.

TIMURKAN.

Now, pious falfe one, fay, who is that youth?

ZAMTI.

His air, his features, and his honeft mien
Proclaim all fair within.—But, mighty fir,
I know him not.—

TIMURKAN.

Take heed, old man, nor dare,
As thou do'ft dread my pow'r, to practife guile
Beneath a mafk of facerdotal perfidy:
Prieftcraft, I think, calls it a pious fraud.

ZAMTI.

Prieftcraft and facerdotal perfidy
To me are yet unknown.—Religion's garb
Here never ferves to confecrate a crime;
We have not yet, thank heav'n, fo far imbib'd
The vices of the north.—

TIMURKAN.

TIMURKAN.

Thou vile impoſtor!
Avow Zaphimri, whom thy treach'rous arts
Conceal'd from juſtice; or elſe deſolation
Again ſhall ravage this devoted land.

ZAMTI.

Alas! full well thou know'ſt, that arm already
Hath ſhed all royal blood.——

TIMURKAN.

Traitor, 'tis falſe;——
By thee, vile ſlave, I have been wrought to think
The hated race deſtroy'd—thy artful tale
Abus'd my cred'lous ear.—But know, at length
Some captive ſlaves, by my command impal'd,
Have own'd the horrid truth;—have own'd they
    fought
To ſeat Zaphimri on the throne of China.
Hear me, thou froward boy;—dar'ſt thou be honeſt,
And anſwer who thou art?——

HAMET.

Dare I be honeſt?——
I dare;—a mind grown up in native honour
Dares not be otherwiſe—then if thy troops
Aſk from the lightning of whoſe blade they fled,
Tell 'em 'twas Hamet's.——

ZAMTI.

'Tis—it is my ſon——
My boy,—my Hamet——   *Aſide.*

TIMURKAN.

Where was your abode?——

HAMET.

Far hence remote, in Corea's happy realm——
Where the firſt beams of day with orient bluſhes
Tinge the ſalt wave—there on the ſea-beat ſhore

A cavern'd rock yielded a lone retreat
To virtuous Morat.——

ZAMTI.
Oh! ill-fated youth! *Aside.*

HAMET.
The pious hermit in that mofs-grown dwelling
Found an afylum from heart-piercing woes,
From flav'ry, and that reftlefs din of arms
With which thy fell ambition fhook the world.
There too the fage nurtur'd my greener years;
With him and contemplation have I walk'd
The paths of wifdom; what the great Confucius
Of moral beauty taught,—whate'er the wife,
Still wooing knowledge in her fecret haunts,
Difclos'd of nature to the fons of men,
My wond'ring mind has heard—but above all
The hermit taught me the moft ufeful fcience,
That noble fcience, to be Brave and Good.——

ZAMTI.
Oh! lovely youth—at ev'ry word he utters,
A foft effufion mix'd of grief and joy
Flows o'er my heart. *Aside.*

TIMURKAN,
Who, faid he, was your father?

HAMET.
My birth, the pious fage,—I know not why——
Still wrapp'd in filence; and when urg'd to tell,
He only anfwer'd that a time might come,
I fhould not blufh to know my father.——

TIMURKAN.
Now
With truth declare, haft thou ne'er heard of Zamti?

HAMET.
Of Zamti?—oft enraptur'd with his name

My

My heart has glow'd within me, as I heard
The praises of the godlike man.——

TIMURKAN.   *To* Zamti.

Thou slave,
Each circumstance arraigns thy guilt.——

HAMET.

Oh! heav'ns!
Can that be Zamti!

TIMURKAN.

Yes, that is the traitor——

HAMET.

Let me adore his venerable form,
Thus on my knees adore——

ZAMTI.

I cannot look upon him,
Lest tenderness dissolve my feeble pow'rs,
And wrest my purpose from me——   *Aside.*

TIMURKAN.

Hence, vain boy!
Thou specious traitor, thou false hoary moralist!
                                                To Zamti.
Confusion has o'erta'en thy subtle frauds.
To make my crown's assurance firm, that none
Hereafter shall aspire to wrench it from me,
Now own your fancied king; or, by yon heav'n,
To make our vengeance sure, thro' all the east
Each youth shall die, and carnage thin mankind,
Till in the gen'ral wreck your boasted Orphan
Shall undistinguish'd fall.—Thou know'st my word
Is fate.—Octar, draw near—when treason lurks,
Each moment's big with danger—thou observe
These my commands——
                            Talks apart to Octar.

ZAMTI.

ZAMTI.
Now virtuous cruelty repress my tears.
—Cease your soft conflict, nature. — Hear me,
   Tartar.——
That youth—his air—his ev'ry look, unmans me
   quite.——

TIMURKAN.
Wilt thou begin, dissembler?

ZAMTI.
Down, down, down——
It must be so, or all is lost—That youth,—
I've dealt by him—as ev'ry king could wish
In a like case his faithful subjects would.

TIMURKAN.
Do'st thou then own it?—Triumph, Timurkan,
And in Zaphimri's grave lie hush'd my fears.
Brave Octar, let the victim straight be led
To yonder sacred fane; there, in the view
Of my rejoicing Tartars, the declining sun
Shall see him offered to our living Lama,
For this day's conquest:—thence a golden train
Of radiant years, shall mark my future sway. [*Exit*.

ZAMTI.
Flow, flow my tears, and ease this aching breast.

HAMET.
Nay, do not weep for me, thou good old man.
If it will close the wounds of bleeding China,
That a poor wretch like me must yield his life,
I give it freely.—If I am a king,
Tho' sure it cannot be, what greater blessing
Can a young prince enjoy, than to diffuse,
By one great act, that happiness on millions,
For which his life should be a round of care?
Come, lead me to my fate.— *Exit with* Octar, &c.

ZAMTI.

Hold, hold my heart!
—My gallant, gen'rous youth!—Mandane's air,
His mother's dear resemblance rives my soul.

MANDANE *within.*

Oh! let me fly, and find the barb'rous man—
Where—where is Zamti?——

ZAMTI.

Ha!—'tis Mandane——
Wild as the winds, the mother all alive
In ev'ry heartstring, the forlorn one comes
To claim her boy——

Enter MANDANE.

MANDANE.

And can it then be true?
Is human nature exil'd from thy breast?
Art thou indeed so barb'rous?

ZAMTI.

Lov'd Mandane,
Fix not your scorpions here—a bearded shaft
Already drinks my spirits up.——

MANDANE.

I've seen
The trusty Morat—Oh! I've heard it all.—
He would have shunn'd my steps; but what can
    'scape
The eye of tenderness like mine?—

ZAMTI.

By heav'n
I cannot speak to thee.——

MANDANE.

Think'st thou those tears,
Those false, those cruel tears, will choak the voice
                                              Of

Of a fond mother's love, now stung to madness?
Oh! I will rend the air with lamentations,
Root up this hair, and beat this throbbing breast,
Turn all connubial joys to bitterness,
To fell despair, to anguish and remorse,
Unless my son—

ZAMTI

Thou ever faithful woman,
Oh! leave me to my woes.—

MANDANE.

Give me my child,
Thou worse than Tartar, give me back my son;
Oh! give him to a mother's eager arms,
And let me strain him to my heart.——

ZAMTI.

Heav'n knows
How dear my boy is here.—But our first duty
Now claims attention—to our country's love,
All other tender fondnesses must yield;
—I was a subject ere I was a father.

MANDANE.

You were a savage bred in Scythian wilds,
And humanizing pity never reach'd
Your heart.—Was it for this—oh! thou unkind one,
Was it for this—oh! thou inhuman father,
You woo'd me to your nuptial bed?—So long
Have I then clasp'd thee in these circling arms,
And made this breast your pillow?—Cruel, say,
Are these your vows?—are these your fond endear-
  ments?
Nay, look upon me—if this wasted form,
These faded eyes have turned your heart against me,
With grief for you I wither'd in my bloom.

ZAMTI.

Why wilt thou pierce my heart?

MANDANE.

MANDANE.

Alas! my son,
Have I then bore thee in these matron arms,
To see thee bleed?—Thus do'st thou then return?
This could your mother hope, when first she sent
Her infant exile to a distant clime?
Ah! could I think thy early love of fame,
Would urge thee to this peril?—thus to fall,
By a stern father's will—by thee to die!—
From thee, inhuman, to receive his doom!—
—Murder'd by thee!—Yet hear me, Zamti, hear
    me—
Thus on my knees—I threaten now no more—
'Tis nature's voice that pleads; nature alarm'd,
Quick, trembling, wild, touch'd to her inmost feel-
    ing,
When force would tear her tender young ones from
    her.

ZAMTI.

Nay, seek not with enfeebling fond ideas
To swell the flood of grief—it is in vain—
He must submit to fate.—

MANDANE.

Barbarian! no—   *She rises hastily.*
He shall not die—rather—I prithee, Zamti,
Urge not a grief-distracted woman:—Tremble
At the wild fury of a mother's love.

ZAMTI.

I tremble rather at a breach of oaths.
But thou break thine.—Bathe your perfidious hands
In this life-blood, betray the righteous cause
Of all our sacred kings.

MANDANE.

Our kings!—our kings!
What are the scepter'd rulers of the world?—
Form'd of one common clay, are they not all
Doom'd with each subject, with the meanest slave,

To drink the cup of human woe?—alike
All levell'd by affliction?—Sacred kings!
'Tis human policy sets up their claim.———
Mine is a mother's cause—— mine is the cause
Of husband, wife, and child;—those tend'rest ties!
Superior to your right divine of kings!———

ZAMTI.

Then go, Mandane—thou once faithful woman,
Dear to this heart in vain;—go, and forget
Those virtuous lessons, which I oft have taught thee,
In fond credulity, while on each word
You hung enamour'd.—Go, to Timurkan
Reveal the awful truth.—Be thou spectatress
Of murder'd majesty.—Embrace your son,
And let him lead in shame and servitude
A life ignobly bought.—Then let those eyes,
Those faded eyes, which grief for me hath dimm'd,
With guilty joy reanimate their lustre,
To brighten slavery, and beam their fires
On the fell Scythian murderer.

MANDANE.

And is it thus,
Thus is Mandane known?—My soul disdains
The vile imputed guilt.—No—never—never—
Still am I true to fame. Come lead me hence,
Where I may lay down life to save Zaphimri,
—But save my Hamet too.—Then, then you'll find
A heart beats here, as warm and great as thine.

ZAMTI.

Then make with me one strong, one glorious effort;
And rank with those, who, from the first of time,
In fame's eternal archives stand rever'd,
For conqu'ring all the dearest ties of nature,
To serve the gen'ral weal.———

MANDANE.

That savage virtue
Loses with me its horrid charms.—I've sworn
To save my king.—But should a mother turn
A dire assassin—oh! I cannot bear
The piercing thought.——Distraction, quick di-
    straction
Will seize my brain.——Think thou behold'st my
    Hamet,
The dear, the lovely youth, my blooming hero,—
Think thou behold'st him—See!—My child!—
    My child!
By guards surrounded, a devoted victim.—
Barbarian hold!—Ah! see, he dies! he dies!—
        She faints into Zamti's *arms.*

ZAMTI.

Where is Arsace?—Fond maternal love
Shakes her weak frame—(*Enter* Arsace.) Quickly,
    Arsace, help
This ever-tender creature.—Wand'ring life
Rekindles in her cheek.—Soft, lead her off
To where the fanning breeze in yonder bow'r,
May woo her spirits back.——Propitious heav'n!
Pity the woundings of a father's heart;
Pity my strugglings with this best of women;
Support our virtue:—kindle in our souls
A ray of your divine enthusiasm;
Such as inflames the patriot's breast, and lifts
Th' impassion'd mind to that sublime of virtue,
That even on the rack it feels the good,
Which in a single hour it works for millions,
And leaves the legacy to after times.
        [*Exit, leading off* Mandane.

End of the Second ACT.

ACT III.

SCENE *a Temple. Several tombs up and down the stage.*

Enter MORAT.

THIS is the place —— these the long winding isles,
The solemn arches, whose religious awe
Attunes the mind to melancholy musing,
Such as befits free men reduc'd to slaves——
Here Zamti meets his friends——amid these tombs,
Where lie the sacred manes of our kings,
They pour their orisons——hold converse here
With the illustrious shades of murder'd heroes;
And meditate a great revenge——*(a groan is heard)*
    a groan!
The burst of anguish from some care-worn wretch
That sorrows o'er his country——ha! 'tis Zamti!

ZAMTI *comes out of a tomb.*
ZAMTI.
Who's he, that seeks these mansions of the dead?
MORAT.
The friend of Zamti and of China.——
ZAMTI.
Morat!
Come to my arms, thou good, thou best of men.——
I have been weeping o'er the sacred reliques

Of a dear murder'd king——Where are our friends?
Haſt ſeen Oraſming?

MORAT.

Thro' theſe vaults of death
Lonely he wanders,——plung'd in deep deſpair.—

ZAMTI.

Haſt thou not told him?—haſt thou nought reveal'd
Touching Zaphimri?

MORAT.

There I wait thy will.——

ZAMTI.

Oh! thou art ever faithful——on thy lips
Sits penſive ſilence, with her hallow'd finger
Guarding the pure receſſes of thy mind.——
But, lo! they come.

Enter ORASMING, ZIMVENTI, *and others.*

ZAMTI.

Droop ye, my gallant friends?

ORASMING.

Oh! Zamti, all is loſt——Our dreams of liberty
Are vaniſh'd into air.——Nought now avails
Integrity of life.——Ev'n heav'n, combin'd
With lawleſs might, abandons us and virtue——

ZAMTI.

Can your great ſouls thus ſhrink within ye? thus
From heroes will ye dwindle into ſlaves?

ORASMING.

Oh! could you give us back Zaphimri!——then
Danger would ſmile, and loſe its face of horror.

ZAMTI.

What,——would his preſence fire ye!

ORASMING.

ORASMING.
'Twould by heav'n!

ZIMVENTI.
This night should free us from the Tartar's yoke.

ZAMTI.
Then mark the care of the all-gracious Gods!
This youthful captive, whom in chains they hold,
Is not Zaphimri.——

ORASMING, ZIMVENTI.
Not Zaphimri!

ZAMTI.
No!
Unconscious of himself, and to the world unknown,
He walks at large among us——

ORASMING.
Heav'nly pow'rs!

ZAMTI.
This night, my friends, this very night to rise
Refulgent from a blow, that frees us all,——
From the usurper's fate!——the first of men,
Deliv'rer of his country!

ORASMING.
Mighty Gods!
Can this be possible?——

ZAMTI.
It is most true——
I'll bring him to ye straight—*(calling to* Etan *within
the tomb)* what ho!——come forth——
You seem transfix'd with wonder—oh! my friends,
Watch all the motions of your rising spirit,
Direct your ardor, when anon ye hear
What fate, long pregnant with the vast event,
Is lab'ring into birth.——

D 3 ETAN

ETAN *comes out of the tomb.*

ETAN.

Each step I move
A deeper horror sits on all the tombs;
Each shrine,——each altar seems to shake; as if
Conscious of some important crisis,——

ZAMTI.

Yes;
A crisis great indeed, is now at hand!——
Heav'n holds its golden balance forth, and weighs
Zaphimri's and the Tartar's destiny,
While hov'ring angels tremble round the beam,
Hast thou beheld that picture?

ETAN.

Fix'd attention
Hath paus'd on ev'ry part; yet still to me
It shadows forth the forms of things unknown;——
All imag'ry obscure, and wrapp'd in darkness,

ZAMTI.

That darkness my informing breath shall clear,
As morn dispels the night. Lo! here display'd
This mighty kingdom's fall.——

ETAN.

Alas! my father,
At sight of these sad colourings of woe,
Our tears will mix with honest indignation.

ZAMTI.

Nay, but survey it closer——see that child,
That royal infant, the last sacred relict
Of China's ancient line——see where a mandarine
Conveys the babe to his wife's fost'ring breast,
There to be nourish'd in an humble state;
While their own son is sent to climes remote;
That, should the dire usurper e'er suspect

The

The prince alive, he in his ftead might bleed,
And mock the murd'rer's rage.——

ETAN.
Amazement thrills
Thro' all my frame, and my mind, big with wonder,
Feels ev'ry pow'r fufpended.——

ZAMTI.
Rather fay
That ftrong imagination burns within thee.——
Do'ft thou not feel a more than common ardor?——

ETAN.
By heav'n my foul dilates with fome new impulfe;
Some ftrange infpir'd emotion——would the hour
Of fate were come——this night my dagger's hilt
I'll bury in the tyrant's heart.——

ZAMTI.
Wilt thou?

ETAN.
By all the mighty dead, that round us lie,
By all who this day groan in chains, I will.

ZAMTI.
And when thou doft,—then tell him 'tis the prince
That ftrikes.——

ETAN.
The prince's wrongs fhall nerve my arm
With tenfold rage.

ZAMTI.
Nay, but the prince himfelf!

ETAN.
What fays my father?——

ZAMTI.
Thou art China's Orphan;
The laft of all our kings——no longer Etan,
But now Zaphimri!

ZAPHIMRI.
Ha!
ORASMING.
O wond'rous hand
Of heav'n!

ZAPHIMRI.
A crowd of circumstances rise——
Thy frequent hints obscure——thy pious care
To train my youth to greatness.—Lend your aid
To my astonish'd pow'rs, that feebly bear
This unexpected shock of royalty.

ZAMTI.
Thou noble youth, now put forth all your strength,
And let heav'n's vengeance brace each sinew.——

ZAPHIMRI.
Vengeance!——
That word has shot its light'ning thro' my soul.—
But tell me, Zamti—still 'tis wonder all——
Am I indeed the Royal Orphan?———

ZAMTI.
Thou;———
Thou art the king, whom as my humble son,
I've nurtur'd in humanity and virtue.
Thy foes could never think to find thee here,
Ev'n in the lion's den; and therefore here
I've fix'd thy safe asylum, while my son
Hath dragg'd his life in exile.—Oh! my friends,
Morat will tell ye all,—each circumstance——
Mean time——there is your king!——
All kneel to him.

ORASMING, ZIMVENTI.
Long live the Father of the eastern world!

ZAMTI.
Sole governor of earth!——

ZAPHIMRI.

ZAPHIMRI.

All-ruling pow'rs!——
Is then a great revenge for all the wrongs
Of bleeding China; are the fame and fate
Of all posterity included here
Within my bosom?—— *They all rise.*

ZAMTI.

Yes; they are; the shades
Of your great ancestors now rise before thee,
Heroes and demi-gods!—— Aloud they call
For the fell Tartar's blood——

ZAPHIMRI.

Oh! Zamti; all
That can alarm the pow'rs of man, now stirs
In this expanding breast.——

ZAMTI.

Anon to burst
With hideous ruin on the foe.——My gallant heroes,
Are our men station'd at their posts?

ORASMING.

They are.——

ZAMTI.

Is ev'ry gate secur'd?

ORASMING.

All safe.——

ZAMTI.

The signal fix'd?——

ORASMING.

It is:—Will Mirvan join us?

ZAMTI.

Doubt him not.——
In bitterness of soul he counts his wrongs,
And pants for vengeance——would have join'd ye
    here,

                                        But,

But, favour'd as he is, his post requires him
About the Tartar's person.—The assault begun,
He'll turn his arms upon th' astonish'd foe,
And add new horrors to the wild commotion.

ZAPHIMRI.

Now, bloody spoiler, now thy hour draws nigh,
And ere the dawn thy guilty reign shall end.

ZAMTI.

How my heart burns within me!—Oh! my friends,
Call now to mind the scene of desolation,
Which Timurkan, in one accursed hour,
Heap'd on this groaning land.—Ev'n now I see
The savage bands, o'er reeking hills of dead,
Forcing their rapid way.—I see them urge
With rage unhallow'd to this sacred temple,
Where good Osmingti, with his queen and children,
Fatigu'd the Gods averse.—See where Arphisa,
Rending the air with agonizing shrieks,
Tears her dishevell'd hair: Then, with a look
Fix'd on her babes, grief choaks its passage up,
And all the feelings of a mother's breast
Throbbing in one mix'd pang, breathless she faints
Within her husband's arms.—Adown his cheek,
In copious streams fast flow'd the manly sorrow;
While clust'ring round his knees his little offspring,
In tears all-eloquent, with arms outstretch'd,
Sue for parental aid.—

ZAPHIMRI.

Go on—the tale
Will fit me for a scene of horror.—

ZAMTI.

Oh! my prince,
The charge, which your great father gave me, still
Sounds in my ear.—Ere yet the foe burst in,
" Zamti," said he—Ah! that imploring eye!—
                                                    That

That agonizing look!——
" Preferve my little boy, my cradled infant——
" Shield him from ruffians——Train his youth to
    " virtue:——
" Virtue will rouze him to a great revenge;
" Or failing—Virtue fhall ftill make him happy."
He could no more—the cruel fpoiler feiz'd him,
And dragg'd my king—my ever honour'd king,—
The father of his people,—bafely dragg'd him
By his white rev'rend locks, from yonder altar,
Here,—on the blood-ftain'd pavement; while the
    queen,
And her dear fondlings, in one mangled heap,
Died in each other's arms.——

        ZAPHIMRI.
Revenge! Revenge!
With more than lion's nerve I'll fpring upon him,
And at one blow relieve the groaning world.
Let us this moment carry fword and fire
To yon devoted walls, and whelm him down
In ruin and difmay.——

        ZAMTI.
Zaphimri no.——
By rafhnefs you may marr a noble caufe.——
To you, my friends, I render up my charge——
To you I give your king.—Farewell, my fov'reign.—

        ZAPHIMRI.
Thou good, thou godlike man—a thoufand feelings
Of warmeft friendfhip—all the tendencies
Of heart-felt gratitude are ftruggling here,
And fain would fpeak to thee, my more than father.
—Farewell;—fure we fhall meet again.——

        ZAMTI.
We fhall——

        ZAPHIMRI.
Farewell—Zamti, farewell. (*Embraces him*) Oraf-
    ming, now

The nobleſt duty calls us.—Now remember
We are the men, whom from all human kind
Our fate hath now ſelected, to come forth
Aſſerters of the public weal;—to drench our ſwords
In the oppreſſor's heart;—to do a deed
Which heav'n, intent on its own holy work,
Shall pauſe with pleaſure to behold.——
[*Exit, with conſpirators.*

ZAMTI.

May the Moſt High
Pour down his bleſſings on him; and anon,
In the dead waſte of night, when awful juſtice
Walks with her crimſon ſteel o'er ſlaughter'd heaps
Of groaning Tartars, may he then direct
His youthful footſteps thro' the paths of peril;
Oh may he guide the horrors of the ſtorm,
An Angel of your wrath, to point your vengeance
On ev'ry guilty head.——Then,—then 'twill be
      enough,
When you have broken the oppreſſor's rod,
Your reign will then be manifeſt—Mankind will ſee
That truth and goodneſs ſtill obtain your care——

A dead march.

What mean thoſe deathful ſounds?—Again!——
      They lead
My boy to ſlaughter—Oh! look down, ye heavens!
Look down propitious!—Teach me to ſubdue
That nature which ye gave.—— [*Exit.*

A dead march. Enter HAMET, OCTAR,
guards, &c.

OCTAR.

Here let the victim fall, and with his blood
Waſh his forefathers' tomb. — Here ends the hated
      race.——
The eaſtern world thro' all her wide domain,
                                                Shall

Shall then submissive feel the Scythian yoke,
And yield to Timurkan.——

 HAMET. *Standing by the tomb.*

Where is the tyrant?—I would have him see,
With envy see, th' unconquer'd pow'r of virtue;
How it can calmly bleed, smile on his racks,
And with strong pinion soar above his pow'r,
To regions of perennial day.——

   OCTAR.

The father
Of the whole eastern world shall mark thee well,
When at to-morrow's dawn thy breathless corse
Is born thro' all our streets for public view.
It now befits thee to prepare for death.

   HAMET.

I am prepar'd.—I have no lust or rapine,
No murders to repent of.——Undismay'd
I can behold all-judging heav'n, whose hand
Still compassing its wond'rous ends, by means
Inextricable to all mortal clue,
Hath now inclos'd me in its awful maze.
Since 'tis by your decree that thus beset
Th' inexorable angel hovers o'er me,
Be your great bidding done.——

   OCTAR.

The sabre's edge
Thirsts for his blood—then let its light'ning fall
On his aspiring head.—— *Guards seize* Hamet.

  MANDANE, *within.*

Off,—set me free.—Inhuman, barb'rous ruffians.—

   OCTAR.

What means that woman with dishevell'd hair,
And wild extravagance of woe?——

       MANDANE.

MANDANE.

My griefs
Scorn all reſtraint—I muſt—I will have way.——
   She enters, and throws herſelf on her knees.
Me,—me, on me convert your rage—plunge deep,
Deep in this boſom your abhorred ſteel,
But ſpare his precious life.——

OCTAR.

Hence, quickly bear
This wild, this frantic woman.——

MANDANE.

Never, never——
You ſhall not force me hence. Here will I cling
Faſt to the earth, and rivet here my hands,
In all the fury of the laſt deſpair.
He is my child,——my dear, dear ſon.——

OCTAR.

How, woman!
Saidſt thou your ſon?——

MANDANE.

Yes, Octar, mine;—my ſon,
My boy,—my Hamet *(ſhe riſes, and embraces him.)*
  Let my eager love
Fly all unbounded to him — oh! my child!—my
  child!——

OCTAR.

Suſpend the ſtroke, ye miniſters of death,
Till Timurkan hear of this new event.
Mean time, thou Mirvan, ſpeed in queſt of Zamti,
And let him anſwer here this wond'rous tale. [*Exit.*

MIRVAN.

The time demands his preſence; or deſpair
May wring each ſecret from her tender breaſt. *Aſide.*
And then our glorious, fancied pile of freedom,
At one dire ſtroke, ſhall tumble into nought.
        [*Exit.*

MANDANE.

MANDANE.

Why did'st thou dare return?—ah! rather why
Did'st thou so long defer with ev'ry grace,
And ev'ry growing virtue, thus to raise
Your mother's dear delight to rapture?

HAMET.

Lost
In the deep mists of darkling ignorance,
To me my birth's unknown—but sure that look,
Those tears, those shrieks, that animated grief
Defying danger, all declare th' effect
Of nature's strugglings in a parent's heart.
Then let me pay my filial duty here,
Kneel to her native dignity, and pour
In tears of joy the transport of a son.——

MANDANE.

Thou art, thou art my son—thy father's face,
His ev'ry feature, blooming in his boy.
Oh! tell me, tell me all; how hast thou liv'd
With faithful Morat?—how did he support
In dreary solitude thy tender years?——
How train thy growing mind? — oh! quickly tell me,
Oh! tell me all, and charm me with thy tongue.

HAMET.

Mysterious pow'rs! have I then liv'd to this,
In th' hour of peril thus to find a parent,
In virtue firm, majestic in distress,
At length to feel unutterable bliss
In her dear circling arms ——   *They embrace.*

Enter TIMURKAN, OCTAR, *&c.*

TIMURKAN.

Where is this wild
Outrageous woman, who with headlong grief
                                    Suspends

Suspends my dread command—tear 'em asunder,—
Send her to some dark cell to rave and shriek
And dwell with madness—and let instant death
Leave that rash youth a headless trunk before me.

MANDANE.

Now by the ever-burning lamps that light
Our holy shrines, by great Confucius' altar,
By the prime source of life, and light, and being,
That is my child, the blossom of my joys——
Send for his cruel father,—he—'tis he
Intends a fraud—he, for a stranger's life,
Would yield his offspring to the cruel ax,
And rend a wretched mother's brain with madness.

Enter ZAMTI.

Sure the sad accents of Mandane's voice
Struck on my frighted sense.——

TIMURKAN.

Once more, thou slave!——
Who is that stubborn youth?

ZAMTI.

Alas! what needs
This iteration of my griefs?

MANDANE.

Oh! horror!—horror!
Thou marble-hearted father!—'tis your child,
And would'st thou see him bleed?——

ZAMTI.

On him!——on him
Let fall your rage, and ease my soul at once
Of all its fears.——

MANDANE.

Oh! my devoted child!   *She faints.*

HAMET.

HAMET.

Support her, heav'n! support her tender frame—
Now, tyrant, now I beg to live—*(kneels)* lo! here
I plead for life;—not for the wretched boon
To breathe the air, which thy ambition taints;—
But oh! to ease a mother's pains;—for her,
For that dear object,—oh! let me live for her.

TIMURKAN.

Now by the conquests this good sword has won,
In her wild vehemence of grief I hear
The genuine voice of nature.

MANDANE, *recovering*.

Ah!——where is he?
He is my son—my child—and not Zaphimri—
Oh! let me clasp thee to my heart——thy hard,
Thy cruel father shall not tear thee from me.——

TIMURKAN.

Hear me, thou frantic mourner, dry those tears—
Perhaps you still may save this darling son.—

MANDANE.

Ah! quickly name the means.———

TIMURKAN,

Give up your king,
Your phantom of a king, to sate my vengeance.

HAMET.

Oh! my much honour'd mother, never hear
The base, the dire proposal—let me rather
Exhaust my life-blood at each gushing vein.
Mandane then,—then you may well rejoice
To find your child,—then you may truly know
The best delight a mother's heart can prove,
When her son dies with glory.———

TIMURKAN.

Curses blast
The stripling's pride—— *Talks apart with* Octar.

ZAMTI.

Ye venerable host,
Ye mighty shades of China's royal line,
Forgive the joy that mingles with my tears,
When I behold him still alive.—Propitious pow'rs!
You never meant entirely to destroy
This bleeding country, when your kind indulgence
Lends us a youth like him.——
Oh! I can hold no more—let me infold
That lovely ardor in his father's arms——
My brave,—my gen'rous boy!—— *Embraces him.*

TIMURKAN.

Dost thou at length
Confess it, traitor?——

ZAMTI.

Yes, I boast it, tyrant;
Boast it to thee,—to earth and heav'n I boast,
This,——this is Zamti's son.——

HAMET.

At length the hour,
The glorious hour is come, by Morat promis'd,
"When Hamet shall not blush to know his father."
Kneels to him.

ZAMTI.

Oh! thou intrepid youth!—what bright reward
Can your glad sire bestow on such desert?——
The righteous Gods, and your own inward feelings
Shall give the sweetest retribution.—Now,
Mandane, now my soul forgives thee all,
Since I have made acquaintance with my son;
Thy lovely weakness I can now excuse;
But oh! I charge thee by a husband's right——

TIMURKAN.

TIMURKAN.

A husband's right!—a traitor has no right——
Society disclaims him——Woman, hear——
Mark well my words——discolour not thy soul
With the black hue of crimes like his——renounce
All hymeneal vows, and take again
Your much lov'd boy to his fond mother's arms,
While justice whirls that traitor to his fate.

MANDANE.

Thou vile adviser!——what, betray my lord,
My honour'd husband——turn a Scythian wife!
Forget the many years of fond delight,
In which my soul ne'er knew decreasing love,
Charm'd with his noble, all-accomplish'd mind!
No, tyrant, no;——with him I'll rather die;
With him in ruin more supremely blest,
Than guilt triumphant on its throne.——

ZAMTI.

Now then,
Inhuman Tartar, I defy thy pow'r——
Lo! here, the father, mother, and the son!
Try all your tortures on us——here we stand
Resolv'd to leave a tract of bright renown
To mark our beings————all resolv'd to die
The votaries of honour!————

TIMURKAN.

Then die ye shall—what ho!—guards, seize the slaves,
Deep in some baleful dungeon's midnight gloom
Let each apart be plung'd—and Etan too—
Let him be forthwith found—he too shall share
His father's fate.————

MIRVAN.

Be it my task, dread sir,
To make the rack ingenious in new pains,

Till even cruelty almoſt relent
At their keen, agonizing groans.————

TIMURKAN.

Be that,
Mirvan, thy care.—Now by th' immortal Lama
I'll wreſt this myſt'ry from 'em—elſe the dawn
Shall ſee me up in arms—'gainſt Corea's chief
I will unfurl my banners—his proud cities
Shall dread my thunder at their gates, and mourn
Their ſmoaking ramparts—o'er his verdant plains
And peaceful vales I'll drive my warlike carr,
And deluge all the eaſt with blood.———   [*Exit.*

OCTAR.

Mirvan, do thou bear hence thoſe miſcreant ſlaves.
Thou, Zamti, art my charge—*Laying hold of him.*

ZAMTI.

Willing I come—   *Shakes him off.*
The ſteady mind can ſcorn your manſions drear,
And brighten horror with its noon-tide ray.
Mandane, ſummon all thy ſtrength.—My ſon,
Thy father doubts not of thy fortitude.
                [*Exit, guarded by* Octar.

MANDANE.

Allow me but one laſt embrace— *To the guards.*

HAMET.

Oh! mother,
Would I could reſcue thee.———

MANDANE.

Loſt, loſt again!

HAMET.

Inhuman, bloody Tartars.
            Both together.
Oh! farewell.——— [*Exeunt, on different ſides.*

End of the Third ACT.

ACT

ACT IV.

SCENE, *a Prison.* HAMET *in chains.*

Enter ZAPHIMRI *(disguised in a Tartar dress)*
with MIRVAN.

MIRVAN.

HERE stretch'd at length on the dank ground he lies;
Scorning his fate.—Your meeting must be short.——

ZAPHIMRI.

It shall.——

MIRVAN.

And yet I tremble for th' event;——
Why would'st thou venture to this place of danger?

ZAPHIMRI.

And can'st thou deem me then so mean of spirit,
To dwell secure in ignominious safety;
With cold insensibility to wait
The ling'ring hours, with coward patience wait 'em,
Deliberating on myself, while ruin
Nods over Zamti's house?

MIRVAN.

Yet whilst thou'rt here,
Thy fate's suspended on each dreadful moment.

ZAPHIMRI.

I will hold converse with him! ev'n tho' death
Were arm'd against the interview.—[*Exit* Mirvan.

HAMET, *still on the ground.*
—What wouldst thou, Tartar?

ZAPHIMRI.
Rise, noble youth,—no vulgar errand mine——

HAMET, *comes forward.*
Now speak thy purpose.——

ZAPHIMRI.
Under this disguise——

HAMET,
If under that disguise, a murd'rer's dagger
Thirst for my blood——thus I can meet the blow.
Throwing himself open.

ZAPHIMRI.
No ruffian's purpose lurks within this bosom.
To these lone walls, where oft the Scythian stabber
With murd'rous stride hath come; these walls that oft
Have seen th' assassin's deeds; I bring a mind
Firm, virtuous, upright.——Under this vile garb,
Lo! here a son of China.—— *Opens his dress.*

HAMET.
Yes, thy garb
Denotes a son of China; and those eyes
Roll with no black intent.——Say on——

ZAPHIMRI.
Inflam'd with admiration of heroic deeds,
I come to seek acquaintance with the youth,
Who for his king would bravely die.——

HAMET.
Say then,
Dost thou applaud the deed?——

ZAPHIMRI.
By heav'n, I do.——

Yes,

Yes, virtuous envy rises in my soul———
Thy ardor charms me, and ev'n now I pant
To change conditions with thee.———

HAMET.

Then my heart
Accepts thy proffer'd friendship;——— in a base,
A prone, degen'rate age, when foreign force,
And foreign manners have o'erwhelm'd us all,
And sunk our native genius;———thou retain'st
A sense of ancient worth.———But wherefore here,
To this sad mansion, this abode of sorrow,
Com'st thou to know a wretch that soon must die?

ZAPHIMRI.

By heav'n, thou shalt not die———I come to speak
The gladsome tidings of a happier fate.———
By me Zaphimri sends———

HAMET.

Zaphimri sends!
Kind pow'rs!———Where is the king?———

ZAPHIMRI.

His steps are safe;
Unseen as is the arrow's path.———By me he says,
He knows, he loves, he wonders at thy virtue.—
By me he swears, rather than thou should'st fall,
He will emerge from dark obscurity,
And greatly brave his fate.———

HAMET.

Ha!—die for me!
For me, ignoble in the scale of being;
An unimportant wretch!———Whoe'er thou art,
I prithee, stranger, bear my answer back———
Oh! tell my sov'reign that here dwells a heart
Superior to all peril.—When I fall,
A worm,—an insect dies!—But in his life
Are wrapp'd the glories of our ancient line,

The liberties of China!—Then let him
Live for his people—Be it mine to die.

ZAPHIMRI.

Can I bear this, ye pow'rs, and not diſſolve
In tears of gratitude and love?——— *Aſide.*

HAMET.

Why ſtreams
That flood of grief?—and why that ſtifled groan?
Thro' the dark miſt his ſorrow caſts around him,
He ſeems no common man.—Say, gen'rous youth,
Who, and what art thou?———

ZAPHIMRI.

Who, and what am I!———
Thou lead'ſt me to a precipice, from whence
Downward to look, turns wild the mad'ning brain,
Scar'd at th' unfathomable deep below.———
Who, and what am I!—Oh! the verieſt wretch
That ever yet groan'd out his ſoul in anguiſh.
One loſt, abandon'd, hopeleſs, plung'd in woe
Beyond redemption's aid.———To tell thee all
In one dire word, big with the laſt diſtreſs,
In one accumulated term of horror,———
———Zaphimri!———

HAMET.

Said'ſt thou!———

ZAPHIMRI.

He!———that fatal wretch;
Exalted into miſery ſupreme.
Oh! I was happy, while good Zamti's ſon
I walk'd the common tracts of life, and ſtrove
Humbly to copy my imagin'd ſire.
But now———

HAMET.

Yes now—if thou art He———as ſure

'Tis

'Tis wond'rous like—rais'd to a ſtate, in which
A nation's happineſs on thee depends.

ZAPHIMRI.

A nation's happineſs!—There, there I bleed—
There are my pangs.—For me this war began ——
For me hath purple ſlaughter drench'd yon fields—
I am the cauſe of all.—I forg'd thoſe chains——
For Zamti and Mandane too—Oh! heav'ns!——
Them have I thrown into a dungeon's gloom.——
Theſe are the horrors of Zaphimri's reign.——
—I am the tyrant!—— I aſcend the throne
By trampling on the neck of innocence;
By baſe ingratitude; by the vile means
Of ſelfiſh cowardice, that can behold
Thee, and thy father, mother, all in chains,
All loſt, all murder'd, that I thence may riſe
Inglorious to a throne!——

HAMET.

Alas! thy ſpirit,
Thy wild diſorder'd fancy pictures forth
Ills, that are not —— or, being ills, not worth
A moment's pauſe.——

ZAPHIMRI.

Not ills!——thou can'ſt not mean it.——
Oh! I'm environ'd with the worſt of woes;——
The angry fates, amidſt their hoards of vengeance,
Had nought but this——they meant to render me
Peculiarly diſtreſs'd. —— Tell me, thou gallant
  youth,——
—A ſoul like thine knows ev'ry fine emotion,——
Is there a nerve, in which the heart of man
Can prove ſuch torture, as when thus it meets
Unequall'd friendſhip, honour, truth, and love,
And no return can make?——Oh! 'tis too much,
Ye mighty Gods, too much—thus, thus to be
A feeble prince, a ſhadow of a king,

Without

Without the pow'r to wreak revenge on guilt,——
—Without the pow'r of doing virtue right.——
HAMET.
That power will come,——
ZAPHIMRI.
But when?———when thou art loft,——
When Zamti and Mandane are deftroy'd——
Oh! for a dagger's point, to plunge it deep,
Deep in this—ha!—Deep in the tyrant's heart.—
HAMET.
There your revenge fhould point.—For that great
    deed
Heav'n hath watch'd all thy ways; and wilt thou
    now
With headlong rage fpurn at its guardian care,
Nor wait the movements of eternal Juftice!——
ZAPHIMRI.
Ha!—whither has my phrenzy ftray'd?——Yes,
    heav'n
Has been all-bounteous.—Righteous pow'rs!——
To you my orifons are due —— But oh!
Complete your goodnefs: —— Save this valiant
    youth;——
Save Zamti's houfe; and then,—if fuch your will,
That from the Tartar's head my arm this night
Shall grafp the crown of China —— teach me then
To bear your dread vicegerency —— I ftand
Refign'd to your high will.——
HAMET.
And heav'n, I truft,
Will ftill preferve thee; in its own good time
Will finifh its decrees.——
ZAPHIMRI.
Yes, Hamet, yes;
A gleam of hope remains.——Should Timurkan
Defer his murder to the midnight hour,
Then

Then will I come,—then burſt theſe guilty walls,
Rend thoſe vile manacles, and give thee freedom.
HAMET.
Oh! no—you muſt not riſk——
ZAPHIMRI.
A band of heroes
For this are ready; honourably leagu'd
To vindicate their rights.——Thy father's care
Plann'd and inſpir'd the whole.—Among the troops,
Nay in his very guards, there are not wanting
Some gallant ſons of China, in that hour,
Who will diſcover their long-pent-up fury,
And deal deſtruction round.——
HAMET.
What—all conven'd,
And ev'ry thing diſpos'd?
ZAPHIMRI.
Determin'd!——Now
In ſilent terror all intent they ſtand,
And wait the ſignal in each gale that blows.
HAMET.
Why did'ſt thou venture forth?
ZAPHIMRI.
What, poorly lurk
While my friends die!—that thought—but, gene-
 rous youth,
I'll not think meanly of thee—No—that thought
Is foreign to thy heart.
HAMET.
But think, my prince,
On China's wrongs, the dying heroes' groans;
Think on thy anceſtors.——
ZAPHIMRI.
My anceſtors!
What is't to me a long-deſcended line,
A race of worthies, legiſlators, heroes,——
—Unleſs I bring their virtues too?—No more—
Thy

Thy own example fires me.——Near this place
I'll take my stand, and watch their busy motions,
Until the gen'ral roar;—then will I come,
And arm thee for th' assault.——

HAMET.

Oh! if thou do'st,
Yet once again I'll wield the deathful blade,
And bear against the foe.——

ZAPHIMRI.

Yes, thou and I
Will rush together thro' the paths of death,
Mow down our way, and with sad overthrow
Pursue the Tartar—like two rushing torrents,
That from the mountain's top, 'midst roaring caves,
'Midst rocks and rent-up trees, foam headlong down,
And each depopulates his way.——

A flourish of trumpets.

HAMET.

What means
That sudden and wild harmony?——

ZAPHIMRI.

Even now
The conqu'ror, and his fell barbaric rout,
For this day's victory indulge their joy;
Joy soon to end in groans—for all conspires
To forward our design—and lo! the lights
That whilom blaz'd to heav'n, now rarely seen
Shed a pale glimmer, and the foe secure
Sinks down in deep debauch; while all awake,
The genius of this land broods o'er the work
Of justice and revenge.——

HAMET.

Oh! revel on,
Still unsuspecting plunge in guilty joy,
And bury thee in riot.——

ZAPHIMRI.

Ne'er again
To wake from that vile trance—for ere the dawn,
Detested spoiler, thy hot blood shall smoke
On the stain'd marble, and thy limbs abhorr'd
I'll scatter to the dogs of China.——

Enter MIRVAN.

MIRVAN.

Break off your conf'rence—Octar this way comes.

ZAPHIMRI.

This garb will cloak me from each hostile eye;
Thou need'st not fear detection.——

Enter OCTAR.

MIRVAN.

There's your pris'ner.——　　　*Pointing to* Hamet.

OCTAR.

Lead him to where Mandane's matron grief
Rings thro' yon vaulted roof.——

HAMET.

Oh! lead me to her;
Let me give balm to her afflicted mind;
And soften anguish in a parent's breast.
　　　　　　　　　[*Exit, with* Mirvan.

ZAPHIMRI.

What may this mean?—— I dread some lurking
　　mischief.—— [*Exit on the opposite side.*

OCTAR.

When the boy clings around his mother's heart
In fond endearment, then to tear him from her,
Will once again awaken all her tenderness,
And in her impotence of grief, the truth

At

At length will burst its way.—But Timurkan
Impatient comes.———

Enter TIMURKAN.

OCTAR.
Thus with disorder'd looks,
Why will my sov'reign shun the genial banquet,
To seek a dungeon's gloom?

TIMURKAN.
Oh! valiant Octar,
A more than midnight gloom involves my soul.
Hast thou beheld this stubborn Mandarine?

OCTAR.
I have; and tried by ev'ry threaten'd vengeance
To bend his soul: Unconquer'd yet by words
He smiles contempt; as if some inward joy,
Like the sun lab'ring in a night of clouds,
Shot forth its glad'ning unresisted beams,
Chearing the face of woe.———

TIMURKAN.
What of Mandane?———

OCTAR.
At first with tears and bitter lamentations
She call'd on Hamet lost;—but when I urg'd,
She still might save her boy, and save herself,
Would she but give Zaphimri to your wrath,
Her tears forgot to flow;—her voice, her look,
Her colour sudden chang'd, and all her form
Enlarging with th' emotions of her soul,
Grew vaster to the sight.—With blood-shot eyes
She cast a look of silent indignation,
Then turn'd in sullen mood away.

TIMURKAN.
Perdition
O'erwhelm her pride.———

OCTAR.

OCTAR.

Might I advise you, sir,
An artful tale of love should softly glide
To her afflicted soul —— a conqu'ror's sighs
Will waft a thousand wishes to her heart,
Till female vanity aspire to reach
The eastern throne; and when her virtue melts
In the soft tumult of her gay desires,
Win from her ev'ry truth, then spurn to shame
The weak, deluded woman. ——

TIMURKAN.

Octar, no ——
I cannot stoop with love-sick adulation
To thrill in languishing desire, and try
The hopes, the fears, and the caprice of love.
Enur'd to rougher scenes, far other arts
My mind employ'd,—to fling the well-stor'd quiver
Over this manly arm, and wing the dart
At the fleet rain-deer, sweeping down the vale,
Or up the mountain, straining ev'ry nerve;
To vault the neighing steed, and urge his course
Swifter than whirlwinds—thro' the ranks of war
To drive my chariot-wheels, smoaking with gore:
These are my passions, this my only science,
Above the puling sicknesses of love.
Bring that vile slave, the hoary priest, before me.
[*Exit* Octár.

TIMURKAN.

By heav'n their fortitude erects a fence
To shield 'em from my wrath, more pow'rful far
Than their high-boasted wall, which long hath stood
The shock of time, of war, of storms, and thunder,
The wonder of the world! ——
What art thou, Virtue, who can'st thus inspire
This stubborn pride, this dignity of soul,
And still unfading, beauteous in distress,
Can'st taste of joys, my heart hath never known?
Enter

Enter ZAMTI, *in Chains.*

TIMURKAN.

Mark me, thou traitor, thy detested sight
Once more I brook, to try if yet the sense
Of deeds abhorr'd as thine, has touch'd your soul.
Or clear this myst'ry, or by yonder heav'n
I'll hunt Zaphimri to his secret haunt,
Or spread a gen'ral carnage round the world.

ZAMTI.

Thy rage is vain——far from thy ruthless pow'r
Kind heav'n protects him, till the awful truth
In some dread hour of horror and revenge
Shall burst like thunder on thee.——

TIMURKAN.

Ha!——beware,
Nor rouze my lion-rage—yet, ere 'tis late,
Repent thee of thy crimes.——

ZAMTI.

The crime would be
To yield to thy unjust commands.——But know,
A louder voice than thine forbids the deed;
The voice of all my kings!—forth from their tombs
Ev'n now they send a peal of groans to heav'n,
Where all thy murders are long since gone up,
And stand in dread array against thee.

TIMURKAN.

Murders!
Ungrateful Mandarine!——say, did not I,
When civil discord lighted up her brand,
And scatter'd wide her flames; when fierce contention
'Twixt Xohohamti and Zaphimri's father
Sorely convuls'd the realm; did not I then

Lead

Lead forth my Tartars from their northern frontier,
And bid fair order rife?

ZAMTI.

Bid order rife!
Haſt thou not ſmote us with a hand of wrath?
By thee each art has died, and ev'ry ſcience
Gone out at thy fell blaſt——art thou not come
To ſack our cities, to ſubvert our temples,
The temples of our Gods, and with the worſhip,
The monſtrous worſhip of your living Lama,
Profane our holy ſhrines?

TIMURKAN.

Peace, inſolent,
Nor dare with horrid treaſon to provoke
The wrath of injur'd majeſty.——

ZAMTI.

Yes, tyrant,
Yes, thou haſt ſmote us with a hand of wrath;
Full twenty years haſt ſmote us; but at length
Will come the hour of heav'n's juſt viſitation,
When thou ſhalt rue—— hear me, thou man of
    blood——
Yes, thou ſhalt rue the day, when thy fell rage
Imbrued thoſe hands in royal blood——now tremble——
The arm of the Moſt High is bar'd againſt thee——
And ſee!——the hand of fate deſcribes thy doom
In glaring letters on yon rubied wall!——
Each gleam of light is periſh'd out of heav'n,
And darkneſs ruſhes o'er the face of earth.

TIMURKAN.

Think'ſt thou, vile ſlave, with viſionary fears
I e'er can ſhrink appal'd?——thou moon-ſtruck ſeer!
No more I'll bear this mockery of words——
Or ſtrait reſolve me, or, by hell and vengeance,
Unheard-of torment waits thee ——

F   ZAMTI.

ZAMTI.

Know'ſt thou not
I offer'd up my boy?—and after that,
After that conflict, think'ſt thou there is aught
Zamti has left to fear?——

TIMURKAN.

Yes, learn to fear
My will—my ſov'reign will—which here is law,
And treads upon the neck of ſlaves.——

ZAMTI.

Thy will
The law in China!—Ill-inſtructed man!—
Now learn an awful truth,——Tho' ruffian pow'r
May for a while ſuppreſs all ſacred order,
And trample on the rights of man;——the ſoul,
Which gave our legiſlation life and vigour,
Shall ſtill ſubſiſt—above the tyrant's reach.—
—The ſpirit of the laws can never die——

TIMURKAN.

I'll hear no more.—What ho!—*(Enter* Octar, *and
 guards)*—Bring forth Mandane——
Ruin involves ye all—this very hour
Shall ſee your ſon impal'd.—Yes, both your ſons.—
Let Etan be brought forth.——

OCTAR.

Etan, my liege,
Is fled for ſafety.——

TIMURKAN.

Thou pernicious ſlave!   *To* Zamti.
Him too would'ſt thou withdraw from juſtice?——
 —him
Would'ſt thou ſend hence to Corea's realm, to brood
O'er ſome new work of treaſon?—By the pow'rs
Who feel a joy in vengeance, and delight
In human blood, I will unchain my fury

On

On all, who trace Zaphimri in his years;
But chief on thee, and thy devoted race.

Enter MANDANE *and* HAMET.

Mirvan *guarding them, &c.*

TIMURKAN.

Woman, attend my words—instant reveal
This dark conspiracy, and save thyself.—
If wilful thou wilt spurn the joys that woo thee,
The rack shall have its prey.——

MANDANE.

It is in vain.——
I tell thee, Homicide, my soul is bound
By solemn vows; and wouldst thou have me break
What angels wafted on their wings to heav'n?

TIMURKAN.

Renounce your rash resolves, nor court destruction.

MANDANE.

Goddess of vengeance, from your realms above,
Where near the throne of the Most High thou
    dwell'st,
Inspher'd in darkness, amidst hoards of thunder;
Serenely dreadful, 'till dire human crimes
Provoke thee down; now, on the whirlwind's wing
Descend, and with your flaming sword, your bolts
Red with almighty wrath, let loose your rage,
And blast this vile seducer in his guilt.

TIMURKAN.

Blind frantic woman!—think on your lov'd boy.—

MANDANE.

That tender struggle's o'er—if he must die,
I'll greatly dare to follow.——

F 2   TIMURKAN.

TIMURKAN.

Then forthwith
I'll put thee to the proof—Drag forth the boy
To inftant death.—— *They feize* Hamet.

HAMET.

Come on then——Lead me hence
To fome new world where juftice reigns, for here
Thy iron hand is ftretch'd o'er all.——

[*Exit, guarded.*

TIMURKAN.

Quick, drag him forth.

MANDANE.

Now by the pow'rs above, by ev'ry tie
Of humanizing pity, feize me firft;
Oh! fpare my child, and end his wretched mother.

TIMURKAN.

Thou plead'ft in vain.——

Enter a Meffenger in hafte.

Meffenger.

Etan, dread fir, is found.——

ZAMTI.

Ah! China totters on the brink of ruin.   *Afide.*

TIMURKAN.

Where lurk'd the flave?

Meffenger.

Emerging from difguife,
He rufh'd amid the guards that led forth Hamet;
"Sufpend the ftroke," he cry'd; then crav'd ad-
    mittance
To your dread prefence, on affairs, he fays,
Of higheft import to your throne and life.

ZAMTI.

ZAMTI.
Ruin impends. *(aside)* Heed not an idle boy.——
                    To Timurkan.
TIMURKAN.
Yes, I will see him—bring him straight before me.
ZAMTI.
Angels of light, quick on the rapid wing
Dart from the throne of grace, and hover round
 him.

Enter ZAPHIMRI, *guards following him.*

TIMURKAN.
Thou com'st on matters of importance deep
Unto my throne and life.——
ZAPHIMRI.
I do.——This very hour
Thy death is plotting.——
TIMURKAN.
Ha!——by whom?
ZAPHIMRI.
Zaphimri!
ZAMTI.
What means my son?——
TIMURKAN.
Quick, give him to my rage,
And mercy shall to thee extend.——
ZAPHIMRI.
Think not
I meanly come to save this wretched being.——
Pity Mandane—Save her tender frame—*Kneels.*
Pity that youth—oh! save that godlike man.——
ZAMTI.
Wilt thou dishonour me, degrade thyself,

Thy native dignity by basely kneeling?——
Quit that vile posture.——

TIMURKAN.

Rash intruder, hence.—— *To Zamti,*
Hear me, thou stripling;—or unfold thy tale,
Or by yon heav'n they die—Would'st thou appease
    my wrath?
—Bring me Zaphimri's head.——

ZAPHIMRI.

Will that suffice?

ZAMTI.

Oh! heavens! *Aside.*

TIMURKAN.

It will——

ZAPHIMRI.

Then take it, tyrant.
    Rising up, and pointing to himself,

ZAMTI. HAMET.

Ah!

ZAPHIMRI.

I am Zaphimri—I your mortal foe.——

ZAMTI.

Now by yon heav'n! it is not.——

ZAPHIMRI.

Here——strike here——
Since nought but royal blood can quench thy thirst.——
Unsluice these veins,——but spare their matchless
    lives.——

TIMURKAN.

Would'st thou deceive me too?

ZAMTI.

He would——

ZAPHIMRI.

No——here,
Here on his knees, Zaphimri begs to die.

ZAMTI.

ZAMTI.

Oh! horror, 'tis my son—by great Confucius,
That is my Etan, my too gen'rous boy,
That fain would die to save his aged sire.——

MANDANE.

Alas! all's ruin'd—freedom is no more.— *Aside.*

ZAPHIMRI.

Yet hear me, Tartar—hear the voice of truth—
I am your victim—by the gods, I am.——
     Laying hold of Timurkan.

TIMURKAN.

Thou early traitor!—by your guilty sire
Train'd up in fraud—no more these arts prevail.—
My rage is up in arms, ne'er to know rest,
Until Zaphimri perish.—Off, vile slave——
This very moment sweep 'em from my sight.

MANDANE.

Alas! my husband—Oh! my son, my son—

ZAMTI.

May all the host of heav'n protect him still!
    [*Exeunt* Zamti *and* Mandane,
     guarded by Octar, *&c.*

ZAPHIMRI, *struggling with* Timurkan, *on his knees.*

Ah! yet withold—in pity hold a moment——
I am Zaphimri—I resign my crown———

TIMURKAN.

Away, vain boy!—go see them bleed—behold
How they will writhe in pangs;——pangs doom'd
 for thee,
And ev'ry stripling thro' the east.—— Vile slave,
  away!   *Breaks from him, and exit.*

ZAPHIMRI, *lying on the ground; officers and guards behind him.*

Oh! cruel!———yet a moment——Barbarous Scythians!——
Wilt thou not open earth, and take me down,
Down to thy caverns of eternal darkness,
From this supreme of woe?——Here will I lie,
Here on thy flinty bosom,——with this breast
I'll harrow up my grave, and end at once
This pow'rless wretch,—this ignominious king!——
——And sleeps almighty Justice? Will it not
Now waken all its terrors?—arm yon band
Of secret heroes with avenging thunder,
By heaven that thought *(rising)* lifts up my kindling soul
With renovated fire *(aside.)* My glorious friends,
(Who now convene big with your country's fate,)
When I am dead,—oh! give me just revenge——
Let not my shade rise unaton'd amongst ye;——
Let me not die inglorious;——make my fall
With some great act of yet unheard-of vengeance,
Resound throughout the world; that farthest Scythia
May stand appall'd at the huge distant roar
Of one vast ruin tumbling on the heads
Of this fell tyrant, and his hated race.

[*Exit, guarded.*

End of the Fourth ACT.

ACT V.

SCENE, *the Palace.*

Enter OCTAR; ZAMTI *and* MANDANE, *following him.*

ZAMTI.

WHY dost thou lead us to this hated mansion? Must we again behold the tyrant's frown? Thou know'st our hearts are fix'd.—

OCTAR.

The war of words
We scorn again to wage —— hither ye come
Beneath a monarch's eye to meet your doom.
The rack is now preparing—Timurkan
Shall soon behold your pangs, and count each groan
Ev'n to the fullest luxury of vengeance.
Guard well that passage *(to the guards within)*, see
    these traitors find
No means of flight; while to the conqueror
I hasten, to receive his last commands.
       [*Exit* Octar, *on the opposite side.*

ZAMTI *and* MANDANE.

ZAMTI.

Thou ever faithful creature ——

MANDANE.

Can'st thou, Zamti,
Still call me faithful? —— by that honour'd name
                       Wilt

Wilt thou call her, whose mild maternal love
Hath overwhelm'd us all?——

ZAMTI.

Thou art my wife,
Whose matchless excellence, ev'n in bondage,
Hath chear'd my soul; but now thy ev'ry charm,
By virtue waken'd, kindled by distress
To higher lustre, all my passions beat
Unutterable gratitude and love.
And must—oh! cruel!—must I see thee bleed?——

MANDANE.

For me death wears no terror on his brow ——
Full twenty years hath this resounding breast
Been smote with these sad hands; these haggard eyes
Have seen my country's fall; my dearest husband,
My son,—my king,—all in the Tartar's hands:
What then remains for me?—Death,—only death.

ZAMTI.

Ah! can thy tenderness endure the pangs
Inventive cruelty ev'n now designs?——
Must this fair form——this soft perfection bleed?
Thy decent limbs be strain'd with cruel cords,
To glut a ruffian's rage?——

MANDANE.

Alas! this frame,
This feeble texture never can sustain it.
But this—this I can bear—   *Shews a dagger.*

ZAMTI.

Ha!

MANDANE.

Yes!——this dagger!——
Do thou but lodge it in this faithful breast;
My heart shall spring to meet thee.———

ZAMTI.

ZAMTI.

Oh!

MANDANE.

Do thou,
My honour'd lord, who taught'ft me ev'ry virtue,
Afford this friendly, this laft human office,
And teach me now to die. ———

ZAMTI.

Oh! never—— never——
Hence let me bear this fatal inftrument———
Takes the dagger.
What, to ufurp the dread prerogative
Of life and death, and meafure out the thread
Of our own beings!—'Tis the coward's act,
Who dares not to encounter pain and peril——
Be that the practice of th' untutor'd favage;——
Be it the practice of the gloomy north.———

MANDANE.

Muft we then wait a haughty tyrant's nod,
The vaffals of his will?—no—let us rather
Nobly break thro' the barriers of this life,
And join the beings of fome other world,
Who'll throng around our greatly daring fouls,
And view the deed with wonder and applaufe.——

ZAMTI.

Diftrefs too exquifite!———ye holy pow'rs,
If aught below can fuperfede your law,
And plead for wretches, who dare, felf-impell'd,
Rufh to your awful prefence;—oh!—it is not
When the diftemper'd paffions rage! when pride
Is ftung to madnefs; when ambition falls
From his high fcaffolding;—oh! no—if aught
Can juftify the blow, it is when virtue
Has nothing left to do;——— when liberty
No more can breathe at large;—'tis with the groans
Of our dear country when we dare to die.

MANDANE.
Then here at once direct the friendly steel.
ZAMTI.
One last adieu!—now!—ah! does this become
Thy husband's love?—thus with uplifted blade
Can I approach that bosom-bliss, where oft
With other looks than these—oh! my Mandane—
I've hush'd my cares within thy shelt'ring arms?—
MANDANE.
Alas! the loves that hover'd o'er our pillows
Have spread their pinions, never to return,
And the pale fates surround us——
Then lay me down in honourable rest;
Come, as thou art, all hero, to my arms,
And free a virtuous wife——
ZAMTI.
It must be so——
Now then prepare thee—my arm flags and droops
Conscious of thee in ev'ry trembling nerve.
Dashes down the dagger.
By heav'n once more I would not raise the point
Against that hoard of sweets, for endless years
Of universal empire.
MANDANE.
Ha! the fell ministers of wrath——and yet
They shall not long insult us in our woes.
Myself will still preserve the means of death.
Takes up the dagger.

Enter TIMURKAN *and* OCTAR.

TIMURKAN.
Now then, detested pair, your hour is come—
Drag forth these slaves to instant death and torment.
I hate this dull delay; I burn to see them
Gasping in death, and welt'ring in their gore.
MANDANE.

MANDANE.

Zamti, support my steps—with thee to die
Is all the boon Mandane now would crave.
[*Exeunt.*

TIMURKAN *and* OCTAR.

TIMURKAN.

Those rash, presumptuous boys, are they brought
    forth?

OCTAR.

Mirvan will lead the victims to their fate.

TIMURKAN.

And yet what boots their death?—the Orphan lives,
And in this breast fell horror and remorse
Must be the dire inhabitants.——Oh! Octar,
These midnight visions shake my inmost soul.——

OCTAR.

And shall the shad'wings of a feverish brain
Disturb a conqu'ror's breast?——

TIMURKAN.

Octar, they've made
Such desolation here—'tis drear and horrible!——
On yonder couch, soon as sleep clos'd my eyes,
All that yon mad enthusiastic priest
In mystic rage denounc'd, rose to my view;
And ever and anon a livid flash,
From conscience shot, shew'd to my aching sight
The colours of my guilt———
Billows of blood were round me; and the ghosts,
The ghosts of heroes, by my rage destroy'd,
Came with their ghastly orbs, and streaming wounds;
They stalk'd around my bed;—with loud acclaim
They call'd Zaphimri! 'midst the lightning's blaze
Heav'n roll'd consenting thunder o'er my head;
Straight from his covert the youth sprung upon me,
And shook his gleaming steel—he hurl'd me down,
                              Down

Down headlong, down the drear——hold, hold!
    where am I?
Oh! this dire whirl of thought—my brain's on fire—
        OCTAR.
Compose this wild disorder of thy soul.
Your foes this moment die.————

    Enter MIRVAN.

        TIMURKAN.
What would'st thou, Mirvan?
        MIRVAN.
Near to the eastern gate, a slave reports,
As on his watch he stood, a gleam of arms
Cast a dim lustre thro' the night; and straight
The steps of men thick sounded in his ear;
In close array they march'd.
        TIMURKAN.
Some lurking treason!————
What, ho! my arms—ourself will sally forth.——
        MIRVAN.
My liege, their scanty and rash-levied crew
Want not a monarch's sword—the valiant Octar,
Join'd by yon faithful guard, will soon chastise them.
        TIMURKAN.
Then be it so—Octar, draw off the guard,
And bring their leaders bound in chains before me.
                    [*Exit* Octar.

    TIMURKAN *and* MIRVAN.

        MIRVAN.
With sure conviction we have further learn'd
The long-contended truth—Etan's their king—
The traitor Zamti counted but one son;
                          And

And him he sent far hence to Corea's realm,
That should it e'er be known the prince surviv'd,
The boy might baffle justice——
TIMURKAN.
Ha! this moment
Ourself will see him fall.——
MIRVAN.
Better, my liege,
At this dead hour you sought repose—mean time
Justice on him shall hold her course.—Your foes
Else might still urge that you delight in blood.
The semblance of humanity will throw
A veil upon ambition's deeds—'tis thus
That mighty conqu'rors thrive;—and ev'n vice,
When it would prosper, borrows virtue's mien.
TIMURKAN.
Mirvan, thou counsel'st right: beneath a shew
Of public weal we lay the nations waste.
And yet these eyes shall never know repose,
Till they behold Zaphimri perish. Mirvan,
Attend me forth.
MIRVAN.
Forgive, my sov'reign liege,
Forgive my over-forward zeal——I knew
It was not fitting he should breathe a moment:
The truth once known, I rush'd upon the victim,
And with this sabre cleft him to the ground.
TIMURKAN.
Thanks to great Lama!—treason is no more,
And their boy king is dead—Mirvan, do thou
This very night bring me the stripling's head.
Soon as the dawn shall purple yonder east,
Aloft in air all China shall behold it,
Parch'd by the sun, and welt'ring to the wind:
Haste, Mirvan, haste, and sate my fondest wish.
MIRVAN.

MIRVAN.
This hour approves my loyalty and truth. [*Exit.*

TIMURKAN.
Their deep-laid plot hath mifs'd its aim, and Timurkan
May reign fecure——no longer horrid dreams
Shall hover round my couch—the proftrate world
Henceforth fhall learn to own my fov'reign fway.

Enter MIRVAN.

TIMURKAN.
Well, Mirvan, haft thou brought the wifh'd-for pledge?

MIRVAN.
My liege, I fear 'twill ftrike thy foul with horror?

TIMURKAN,
By heav'n the fight will glad my longing eyes.
Oh! give it to me.——

Enter ZAPHIMRI *(a fabre in his hand) and plants himfelf before the tyrant.*

TIMURKAN.
Ha! then all is loft.

ZAPHIMRI.
Now, bloody Tartar, now then know Zaphimri.

TIMURKAN.
Accurfed treafon!—to behold thee thus
Alive before me, blafts my aching eye-balls:
My blood forgets to move — each pow'r dies in me——

ZAPHIMRI.
Well may'ſt thou tremble, well may guilt like thine
Shrink back appall'd ;—for now avenging heav'n
In me ſends forth its miniſter of wrath,
To deal deſtruction on thee.——
TIMURKAN.
Treach'rous ſlave!
'Tis falſe!—with coward-art, a baſe aſſaſſin,
A midnight ruffian on my peaceful hour
Secure thou com'ſt, thus to aſſault a warrior,
Thy heart could never dare to meet in arms.
ZAPHIMRI.
Not meet thee, Tartar!—Ha!—in me thou ſee'ſt
One on whoſe head unnumber'd wrongs thou'ſt
    heap'd——
Elſe could I ſcorn thee, thus defenceleſs.—Yes,
By all my great revenge, could bid thee try each
    ſhape,
Aſſume each horrid form, come forth array'd
In all the terrors of deſtructive guilt;——
But now a dear, a murder'd father calls;
He lifts my arm to rivet thee to earth,
Th' avenger of mankind.
MIRVAN.
Fall on, my prince.
TIMURKAN.
By heav'n, I'll dare thee ſtill; reſign it, ſlave,
Reſign thy blade to nobler hands.
                    Snatches Mirvan's *ſabre.*
MIRVAN.
O! horror!
What ho! bring help.—Let not the fate of China
Hang on the iſſue of a doubtful combat.
TIMURKAN.
Come on, preſumptuous boy.

ZAPHIMRI.

Inhuman regicide!
Now, lawless ravager, Zaphimri comes
To wreak his vengeance on thee. [*Exeunt fighting.*

MIRVAN, *solus.*

Oh! nerve his arm, ye pow'rs, and guide each blow!

To him, enter HAMET.

MIRVAN.

See there!—behold—he darts upon his prey.—

ZAPHIMRI, *within.*

Die, bloodhound, die———

TIMURKAN, *within.*

May curses blast my arm
That fail'd so soon!———

HAMET.

The Tartar drops his point.—
Zaphimri now———

TIMURKAN, *within.*

—Have mercy!——mercy!—oh!

ZAPHIMRI, *within.*

Mercy was never thine—This, fell destroyer,
This, for a nation's groans.———

MIRVAN.

The monster dies;———
He quivers on the ground———Then let me fly
To Zamti and Mandane with the tidings,
And call them back to liberty and joy.
[*Exit* Mirvan.

HAMET *remains; to him* ZAPHIMRI.

ZAPHIMRI.

Now, Hamet, now oppression is no more:
This smoking blade hath drunk the tyrant's blood.

HAMET.
China again is free;—there lies the corse
That breath'd destruction to the world.
ZAPHIMRI.
Yes, there,
Tyrannic guilt, behold thy fatal end,
The wages of thy sins.——

Enter MORAT.
MORAT.
Where is the king?
Revenge now stalks abroad.—Our valiant leaders,
True to the destin'd hour, at once broke forth
From ev'ry quarter on th' astonish'd foe;
Octar is fall'n;—all cover'd o'er with wounds
He met his fate; and still the slaught'ring sword
Invades the city, sunk in sleep and wine.
ZAPHIMRI.
Lo! Timurkan lies levell'd with the dust!
Send forth, and let Orasming strait proclaim
Zaphimri king;—my subjects rights restor'd.
[*Exit* Morat.
Now, where is Zamti? where Mandane?—ha!—
What means that look of wan despair?

Enter MIRVAN.

Oh! dire mischance!
While here I trembled for the great event,
The unrelenting slaves, whose trade is death,
Began their work.—— Nor piety, nor age,
Could touch their felon-hearts —— they seiz'd on Zamti,
And bound him on the wheel — all frantic at the sight,
Mandane plung'd a poniard in her heart,
And at her husband's feet expir'd.———

G 2   HAMET.

HAMET.
Oh! heav'ns!
My mother!——

ZAPHIMRI.
Fatal rashness!——Mirvan, say,
Is Zamti too destroy'd?——

MIRVAN.
Smiling in pangs,
We found the good, the venerable man:
Releas'd from anguish, with what strength remain'd,
He reach'd the couch, where lost Mandane lay;
There threw his mangled limbs;——there, cling-
    ing to the body,
Prints thousand kisses on her clay-cold lips,
And pours his sad lamentings, in a strain
Might call each pitying angel from the sky,
To sympathize with human woe.——

The great folding doors open in the back scene.

ZAPHIMRI.
And see,
See on that mournful bier he clasps her still;
Still hangs upon each faded feature; still
To her deaf ear complains in bitter anguish.
Heart-piercing sight!——

HAMET.
Oh! agonizing scene!

*The corpse is brought forward, Zamti lying on
the couch, and clasping the dead body.*

ZAMTI.
Ah! stay, Mandane, stay,——yet once again
Let me behold the day-light of thy eyes——
Gone, gone, for ever, ever gone——those orbs
That ever gently beam'd, must dawn no more.

ZAPHIMRI.
Are these our triumphs?—these our promis'd joys?

ZAMTI.
The music of that voice recalls my soul.
> [*Rises from the body, and runs eagerly to embrace* Zaphimri; *his strength fails him, and he falls at his feet.*

My prince! my king!
ZAPHIMRI.
Soft, raise him from the ground.
ZAMTI.
Zaphimri!—Hamet too!—oh! bless'd event!
I could not hope such tidings—thee, my prince,
Thee too, my son—I thought ye both destroy'd.
My slow remains of life cannot endure
These strong vicissitudes of grief and joy.
And there—oh! heav'n!—see there, there lies
    Mandane!
HAMET.
How fares it now, my father?
ZAMTI.
Lead me to her——
Is that the ever dear, the faithful woman?
Is that my wife?——and is it thus at length,
Thus do I see thee then, Mandane?——cold,
Alas! death-cold——
Cold is that breast, where virtue from above
Made its delighted sojourn, and those lips
That utter'd heav'nly truth,—pale! pale!—dead,
    dead!   *Sinks on the body.*
Pray ye entomb me with her?——
ZAPHIMRI.
Then take, ye pow'rs, then take your conquests back;
Zaphimri never can survive——
ZAMTI, *raising himself.*
I charge thee live;——
A base desertion of the public weal
Can ne'er become a king——alas! my son,——
(By that dear tender name if once again

Zamti may call thee)—tears will have their way—
Forgive this flood of tenderness——my heart
Melts even now——thou noble youth—this is
The only interview we e'er shall have.——
    ZAPHIMRI.
And will ye then, inexorable pow'rs,
Will ye then tear him from my aching heart?——
    ZAMTI.
The moral duties of the private man
Are grafted in thy soul——oh! still remember
The mean immutable of happiness,
Or in the vale of life, or on a throne,
Is virtue——each bad action of a king
Extends beyond his life, and acts again
Its tyranny o'er ages yet unborn.
To error mild, severe to guilt, protect
The helpless innocent; and learn to feel
The best delight of serving human kind.
Be these, my prince, thy arts; be these thy cares.
And live the father of a willing people.
    HAMET.
Oh! cruel!—see—ah! see!—he dies —— his lips
Tremble in agony—his eye-balls glare——
A death-like paleness spreads o'er all his face.
    ZAPHIMRI.
Is there no help to save so dear a life?
    ZAMTI.
It is too late——I die——alas! I die——
Life harrass'd out, pursu'd with barb'rous art
Thro' ev'ry trembling joint,—now fails at once—
Zaphimri——oh! farewell!——I shall not see
The glories of thy reign——Hamet!—my son—
Thou good young man, farewell—Mandane, yes,
My soul with pleasure takes her flight, that thus
Faithful in death, I leave these cold remains
Near thy dear honour'd clay.—— *Dies.*
    ZAPHIMRI.

ZAPHIMRI.
And art thou gone,
Thou best of men?—then must Zaphimri pine
In ever-during grief, since thou art lost;
Since that firm patriot, whose parental care
Should raise, should guide, should animate my virtues,
Lies there a breathless corse.——

HAMET.
My liege, forbear,——
Live for your people; madness and despair
Belong to woes like mine.——

ZAPHIMRI.
Thy woes, indeed,
Are deep, thou pious youth—yes, I will live,
To soften thy afflictions; to assuage
A nation's grief, when such a pair expires.
Come to my heart:——in thee another Zamti
Shall bless the realm——now let me hence to hail
My people with the sound of peace; that done,
To these a grateful monument shall rise,
With all sepulchral honour——frequent there
We'll offer incense;——there each weeping muse
Shall grave the tributary verse;——with tears
Embalm their memories; and teach mankind,
Howe'er Oppression stalk the groaning earth;
Yet heav'n, in its own hour, can bring relief;
Can blast the tyrant in his guilty pride,
And prove the Orphan's guardian to the last.

FINIS.

TO
M. DE VOLTAIRE.

SIR

A Letter to you from an English author will carry with it the appearance of corresponding with the enemy, not only as the two nations are at present involved in a difficult and important war, but also because in many of your late writings you seem determined to live in a state of hostility with the British nation. Whenever we come in your way, " we are ferocious, we are islanders, we are the people whom your country has taught, we fall behind other nations in point of taste and elegance of composition; the same cause that has witheld from us a genius for painting and music, has also deprived us of the true spirit of Tragedy; and, in short, barbarism still prevails among us."

But, notwithstanding this vein of prejudice, which has discoloured almost all your *fugitive pieces*, there still breathes throughout your writings such a general spirit of Humanity and zeal for the honour of the Republic of Letters, that I am inclined to imagine the author of the English Orphan of China (an obscure islander) may still address you upon terms of amity and literary benevolence.

As I have attempted a Tragedy upon a subject that has exercised your excellent talents, and thus have dared to try my strength in the Bow of ULYSSES, I hold myself in some sort accountable to M. DE VOLTAIRE for the departure I have made from his plan, and the substitution of a new fable of my own.

My first propensity to this story was occasioned by the remarks of an admirable critic * of our own, upon the ORPHAN OF THE HOUSE OF CHAU, preserved to us by the industrious and sensible P. DU HALDE, which, as

* Mr. Hurd, in his Commentary upon Horace.

our learned commentator obferves, amidſt great wildneſs and irregularity, has ſtill ſome traces of reſemblance to the beautiful models of antiquity. In my reflections upon this piece, I imagined I ſaw a blemiſh in the manner of ſaving the Orphan, by the tame reſignation of another infant in his place; eſpecially when the ſubject afforded ſo fair an opportunity to delineate the ſtrugglings of a parent, on ſo trying an occaſion. It therefore occurred to me, if a fable could be framed, in which the Father and the two Young Men might be interwoven with probability and perſpicuity, and not embarraſſed with all the perplexities of a riddle, as, you know, is the caſe of the HERACLIUS of CORNEILLE, that then many ſituations might ariſe, in which ſome of the neareſt affections of the heart might be awakened: but even then I was too conſcious that this muſt be executed in its full force, by a genius very different from myſelf.

In this ſtate of mind, ſir, I heard with pleaſure that M. De VOLTAIRE had produced at Paris his L'ORPHELIN DE LA CHINE: I ardently longed for a peruſal of the piece, expecting that ſuch a writer would certainly ſeize all the ſtriking incidents which might naturally grow out of ſo pregnant a ſtory, and that he would leave no ſource of paſſion unopened. I was in ſome ſort, but not wholly diſappointed: I ſaw M. De VOLTAIRE ruſhing into the midſt of things at once; opening his ſubject in an alarming manner; and, after the narrative relating to GENGISKAN is over, working up his firſt act like a poet indeed.

       Meum qui pectus inaniter angit
Ut Magus.

In the beginning of the ſecond act, he again touches our affections with a maſter-hand; but, like a rower who has put forth all his ſtrength, and ſuddenly ſlackens his exertion, I ſaw, or imagined I ſaw, him give way all at once; the great tumult of the paſſions is over; the

interest wears away; GENGISKAN talks polities; the tenderness of a mother, flying with all the strong impulses of nature to the relief of her child, is thrown into cold unimpassioned narrative; the *role pour l'amoureux* must have its place, and the rough conqueror of a whole people must instantly become *Le Chevalier* GENGISKAN, as errant a lover as ever sighed in the Thuilleries at Paris. Your own words, sir, strongly expressive of that manly and sensible taste, which distinguishes you throughout Europe, occurred to me upon this occasion:
" Quelle place pour la galanterie que le parricide &
" l'inceste, qui désolent une famille, & la contagion qui
" ravage un pais? Et quel exemple plus frapant du ridi-
" cule de notre theatre, & du pouvoir de l'habitude,
" que Corneille d'un côté, qui fait dire à Théfée.——

" Quelque ravage affreux qu'étale ici la Peste;

" L'absence aux vrais amans est encore plus funeste.
" Et moi, qui, soixante ans apres lui, viens faire parler
" une vielle Jocaste d'un viel amour: & tout cela pour
" complaire au goût le plus fade & le plus faux qui ait
" jamais corrompu la literature." Indeed, sir, GENGISKAN, in the very moment of overwhelming a whole nation, usurping a crown, and massacring the royal family, except one infant, whom he is in quest of, appeared to me exactly like the amorous ŒDIPUS in the midst of a destructive plague. " Nunc non erat his lo-
" cus."——How would that noble performance, that *Chef d'œuvre* of your country, the ATHALIE of RACINE, have been defaced by the gallantry of an intrigue, if a tyrant had been introduced to make love to the wife of the high-priest? or if JOAD, entertaining a secret affection for ATHALIE, and being asked what orders he would give relating to the delivery of his country, should answer, " aucune," none at all.——And yet this is the language of a northern conqueror, whining for a Mandarine's wife, who has no power of resisting, and hav-

To M. DE VOLTAIRE.

ing no relation to the royal family, could not, by an intermarriage, strengthen his interest in the crown. But to you, who have told us that Love should reign a very tyrant in Tragedy, or not appear there at all, being unfit for the second place; to you, who have said that NERO should not hide himself behind a tapestry to overhear the conversation of his mistress and his rival; to you, sir, what need I urge these remarks?—To fill up the long career of a tragedy with this episodic love must certainly have been the motive that led you into this error; an error I take the liberty to call it, because I have observed it to be the hackneyed and ineffectual stratagem of many modern writers. Within the compass of my reading, there is hardly a bad man in any play, but he is in love with some very good woman: the scenes that pass between them, I have always remarked, are found dull and unawakening by the audience, even though adorned with all the graces of such composition as yours, of which it is but justice to say, that it bestows embellishments upon every subject.

For me, sir, who only draw in crayons, who have no resource to those lasting colours of imagination with which you set off every thing; a writer such as I am, sir, could not presume to support that duplicity of passion which runs through your piece. I could not pretend, by the powers of style, to suborn an audience in favour of those secondary passages, from which their attention naturally revolts. A plainer and more simple method lay before me. I was necessitated to keep the main object as much as possible before the eye; and therefore it was that I took a survey of my subject, in order to catch at every thing that seemed to me to result with order and propriety from it. A scantiness of interesting business seemed to me a primary defect in the construction of the French ORPHAN OF CHINA, and that I imagined had its source in the early date of your play. By beginning almost "gemino ab ovo," by making the Orphan and the Mandarine's son children in their cradles, it appeared to me that you had stripped yourself of two characters, which might be produced in an amiable light, so as to engage the affections of their auditors, not only for themselves, but consequentially for those also to whom they should stand in any degree of relation. From this conduct I proposed a further advantage, that of effacing the very obvious resemblance to the ANDROMACHE, which now strikes every body in your plan. This last remark I do not urge against accidental and distant coincidencies of sentiment, diction, or fable. Many of the Greek plays, we know, had a family-likeness, such as an OEDIPUS, an ELECTRA, an IPHIGENIA in TAURIS, in AULIS, a MEROPE, &c. But what is a beauty in RACINE, seems in his great successor to be a blemish. In the former, nothing depends on the life of ASTYANAX but what was very natural, the happiness of the mother: in the latter, the fate of a kingdom is grafted upon the fortunes of an infant; and I ask your own feelings, (for no body knows the human heart better) Whether an audience is likely to take any considerable interest in the destiny of a babe, who, when your Zamti has saved him, cannot produce any change, any revolution in the affairs of China? No, sir; the conquered remain in the same abject state of vassalage, and the preservation of the infant king becomes therefore almost uninteresting, certainly unimportant: whereas when the Orphan is grown up to maturity, when he is a moral agent in the piece, when a plan is laid for revenging himself on the destroyers of his family, it then becomes a more pressing motive in the Mandarine's mind; nay, it is almost his duty, in such a case, to sacrifice even his own offspring for the good of his country. In your story, sir, give me leave to say, I do not see what end can be answered by ZAMTI's loyalty: his prospect is at least so distant, that it becomes almost chimerical. And therefore, as history warrants an expulsion of the Tartars; as it was not upon the first inroad, but in process of time and experience, that they learned to incorporate themselves with the conquered, by adopting their laws and customs, I had recourse to my own preconceived notions. Whether I was partially attached to them, or whether my reasonings upon your fable were just, you, sir, and the public, will determine.

You will perceive, sir, in the English Orphan some occasional insertions of sentiment from your elegant performance. To use the expression of the late Mr. DRYDEN, when he talks of BEN JOHNSON's imitation of the ancients, you *will often track me in your snow*. For this I shall make no apology, either to the public or to you: none to the public, because they have applauded some strokes for which I am indebted to you; and none certainly to you, because you are well aware I have in this instance followed the example of many admired writers; BOILEAU, CORNEILLE, and RACINE, in France; and in England, MILTON, Mr. ADDISON, and Mr. POPE. It was finely said by you, (I have read the story, and take it upon trust) when it was objected to the celebrated abbé METASTASIO, as a reproach, that he had frequent transfusions of thought from your writings, "Ah! le cher voleur! il m'a bien embelli." This talent of embellishing I do not pretend to; to avail myself of my reading, and to improve my own productions, is all I can pretend to; and that I flatter myself I have done, not only by transplanting from you, but also from many of the writers of antiquity. If the authorities I have abovementioned were not sufficient, I could add another very bright example, the example of M. De VOLTAIRE, whom I have often tracked, to use the same expression again, in the *snow of Shakespear*. The snow of SHAKESPEAR is but a cold expression; but perhaps it will be more agreeable to you, than a word of greater energy, that should convey a full idea of the astonishing powers of that great man; for we islanders have remarked of late, that M. De VOLTAIRE has a particular satisfaction in descanting on the faults of the most wonderful genius that ever existed since the æra of HOMER, and that too, even then, when he is under obligations to him; insomuch that a very ingenious gentleman of my acquaintance tells me, that whenever you treat the English bard as a drunken savage in your *avant propos*, he always deems it a sure prognostic that your play is the better for him.

If the great scenes of SHAKESPEAR, sir; if his boundless view of all nature, the lawn, the wilderness, the blasted heath, mountains, and craggy rocks, with thunder and lightning on their brows; if these cannot strike the imagination of M. De VOLTAIRE, how can I expect that the studied regularity of my little shrubbery should afford him any kind of pleasure? To drop the metaphor, if the following tragedy does not appear to you a MONSTROUS FARCE, it is all I can reasonably expect. But whatever may be your opinion of it, I must beg that you will not make it the criterion by which you would decide concerning the taste of the English nation, or the present state of literature among us. What you have humbly said of yourself, in order to do honour to your nation, I can assert with truth of the author of the English ORPHAN, that he is one of the worst poets now in this country. It is true, indeed, that the play has been received with uncommon applause; that so elegant a writer as the author of CREUSA and THE ROMAN FATHER was my critic and my friend; and that a great deal of very particular honour has been done me by many persons of the first distinction. But, give me leave to say, they all know the faults of the piece as well as if it had been discussed by the academy of *Belles Let-*

To M. De VOLTAIRE.

tres.——We are a generous nation, sir; and even the faintest approaches to merit, always meet here the warmest encouragement. One thing further I will assure you, in case you should discover any traces of barbarism in the style or fable, That if you had been present at the representation, you would have seen a theatrical splendor conducted with a *bienseance* unknown to the *scene Francoise*; the performers of ZAPHIMRI and HAMET, by their interesting manner, would have made you regret that you had not enriched your piece with two characters, to which a colourist, like you, would have given the most beautiful touches of the pencil, had the idea struck your fancy; and, though a weak state of health deprived the play of so fine an actress as Mrs. CIBBER, you would have beheld in MANDANE a figure that would be an ornament to any stage in Europe, and you would have acknowledged that her Acting promises to equal the elegance of her person: moreover, you would have seen a ZAMTI, whose exquisite powers are capable of adding Pathos and Harmony even to our great SHAKESPEAR, and have already been the chief support of some of your own scenes upon the English stage.

Upon the whole, sir, I beg you will not imagine that I have written this Tragedy in the fond hope of eclipsing so celebrated a writer as M. De VOLTAIRE: I had an humbler motive, *propter amorem quod te imitari aveo.* Could I do that in any distant degree, it would very amply gratify the ambition of,

Sir, your real admirer,
and most humble servant,

London, April 30, 1759.

The AUTHOR of
The ORPHAN of CHINA.

Printed for PAUL VAILLANT.

1. THE Lying Valet, a Comedy, by David Garrick, Esq;
2. Lethe, a dramatic Satire, by David Garrick, Esq;
3. Lilliput, a dramatic Entertainment, in one Act.
4. The Male Coquet, a Farce, in two Acts.

By ARTHUR MURPHY, *Esq.*

5. The Apprentice, a Farce, in two Acts.
6. The Upholsterer, or What News? a Farce, in two Acts.
7. The Orphan of China, a Tragedy, in five Acts.
8. The Desert Island, a dramatic Poem, in three Acts.
9. The Way to Keep Him, a Comedy, in three Acts.
10. The same, in five Acts.
11. All in the Wrong, a Comedy, in five Acts.
12. The Old Maid, a Comedy, in two Acts.
13. No One's Enemy but his Own, a Comedy, in five Acts.
14. What we must all come to, a Comedy, in two Acts.
15. The School for Guardians, a Comedy, in five Acts.
16. The Citizen, a Farce, in two Acts.

By SAMUEL FOOTE, *Esq.*

17. The Knights, a Comedy, in two Acts.
18. The Englishman in Paris, a Comedy, in two Acts.
19. The Englishman returned from Paris, a Farce, in two Acts.
20. The Mayor of Garrett, a Comedy, in two Acts.
21. The Commissary, a Comedy, in three Acts.
22. The Patron, a Comedy, in three Acts.
23. The Lyar, a Comedy, in three Acts.
24. The Lame Lover, a Comedy, in three Acts.
25. Regulus, a Tragedy, in five Acts, by Mr. HAVARD.
26. The Letters of Pliny the Younger, with Observations on each Letter, by JOHN Earl of ORRERY, 2 Vol. Octavo.
27. A new Royal French Grammar, by JOHN PALAIRET, 12mo.
28. A new History of England, in French and English, by Question and Answer. 12mo, a new Edition.

N. B. This Book is intended for the Use of all those who learn the French or English Languages, and is very proper for young Persons at Schools.

29. Nouvelle Histoire d'Angleterre, par Demandes & par Reponses, 12mo.
30. A New French Dictionary, in two Parts; the First French and English, the Second English and French:

CONTAINING,

I. Several HUNDRED WORDS not to be found in any of the Dictionaries hitherto published:
II. The various MEANINGS of Words, often explained by French or English Sentences:
III. The GENDERS of NOUNS, ADJECTIVES, and PRONOUNS, and the CONJUGATIONS of VERBS:
IV. The IRREGULARITIES of the PARTS of SPEECH.

To which is prefixed a French Grammar, shewing how to form the regular Parts of Speech.

By THOMAS DELETANVILLE, Octavo, Price 7 s.

ZENOBIA:

A TRAGEDY.

As it is performed at the

THEATRE ROYAL

IN

DRURY-LANE.

By the AUTHOR of the

ORPHAN OF CHINA.

THE FOURTH EDITION.

LONDON:
Printed for W. GRIFFIN, in Catharine-street, Strand.
MDCCLXVIII.

[P. 1s. 6d.

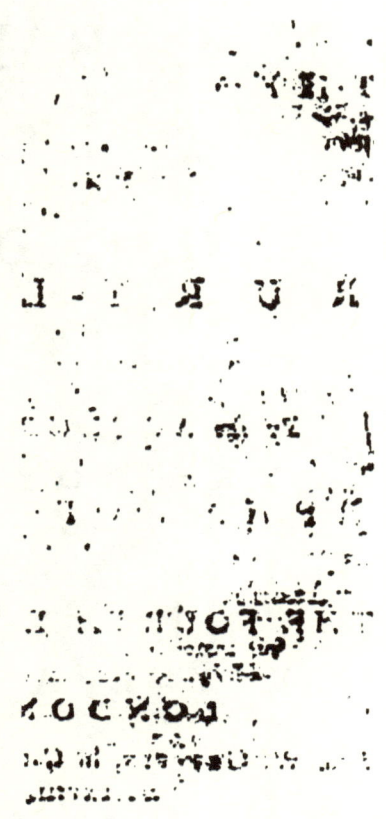

TO
Mrs. DANCER.

MADAM,

IN a country, where addresses of this nature have generally waited upon the Great, upon a Wealthy Merchant, a Rich Commissary, or some New Man from the Sugar-islands, it will appear as surprizing to many, as, no doubt, it will to yourself, that a New Form of Dedication should now be introduced. For the trouble I am giving you it will, however, be unnecessary to make any further apology, when I observe that in France, where talents are honoured, it has been frequently the practice of the most celebrated wits to do justice to those, who, by their profession, are the very Organ of the Muses. A VOLTAIRE and a MARMONTEL have paid their compliments to a CLAIRON: and why may not an English Author, inferior as he is, and ever must be, to writers of that class, rival at least their politeness, by addressing himself to Mrs. DANCER, one of the first Ornaments of the British Theatre?

There are, indeed, I must confess it, some demands upon my gratitude on this occasion, which even now are struggling to call my attention another way. Mr. GARRICK, Madam, has a claim to all the handsome things that can be said of him. His politeness from the moment he saw the play, his assiduity in preparing it for representation, the taste with which he has decorated it, and the warmth of his zeal for the honour of the piece, are circumstances that call upon me for the strongest acknowledgements. I
could

DEDICATION.

could employ my pen with pleasure in thanking Mr. BARRY for the very fine exertion of his powers, wherever the Poet gave the smallest opportunity. Mr. HOLLAND, who had before now given spirit to such scenes as mine, has renewed the obligation. I could add others to the list, but they, and even Mr. GARRICK at their head, must excuse me, if I turn to Mrs. DANCER, and say with *Hamlet*, " Here's metal more attractive."

ZENOBIA, Madam, is your own entirely. Wherever my inaccuracy has left imperfections, they are so happily varnished over by your skill, that either they are not seen, or you extort forgiveness for them: and if the Author is any where lucky enough to *snatch a grace* beyond his usual reach, it is multiplied by your address into a number of beauties, like the SWORD in *Tasso's Jerusalem*, which, when brandished by the hand of *Rinaldo*, appears to the whole army to be THREE SWORDS.

The fate of ZENOBIA has been very extraordinary. She was saved in her life-time from the waters of the *Araxes* by the hand of a shepherd, and now she is saved from the critics by Mrs. DANCER.

In testimony of the fact, the play, Madam, is inscribed to you by him, who admires your talents, and remains

Your most obedient Servant,

THE AUTHOR.

March 3, 1768.

PROLOGUE

Spoken by Mr. HOLLAND.

OF old,—when Rome in a declining age
Of lawless pow'r had felt the barb'rous rage,
This was the tyrant's art:—He gave a prize
To him, who a new pleasure should devise.
 Ye tyrants of the Pit, whose cold disdain
Rejects and nauseates the repeated strain;
Who call for rarities to quicken sense,
Say, do you always the reward dispense?
 Ye bards,---to whom French wit gives kind relief,
Are ye not oft the first —— to cry STOP THIEF!
Say,---to a brother do you e're allow
One little sprig, one leaf to deck his brow?
No;---- fierce invective stuns the play-wright's ears,
Wits, Poets corner, Ledgers, Gazetteers?
'Tis said, the Tartar,---- e're he pierce the heart,
Inscribes his name upon his poison'd dart.
That scheme's rejected by each scribbling spark;
----Our Christian system — stabs you in the dark.
 And yet the desp'rate author of to-night
Dares on the muses wing another flight;
Once more a dupe to fame forsakes his ease,
And feels th' ambition --- here again to please.
 He brings a tale from a far distant age,
Enobled by the grave historic page! *
Zenobia's woes have touch'd each polish'd state;
The brightest eyes of France have mourn'd her fate.
Harmonious Italy her tribute paid,
And sung a dirge to her lamented shade.
 Yet think not that we mean to mock the eye
With pilfer'd colours of a foreign dye.
NOT to translate our bard his pen doth dip;
He takes a play, as Britons take a ship;
They heave her down;--- with many a sturdy stroke,
Repair her well, and build with Heart of Oak.
To ev'ry breeze set Britain's streamers free,
NEW-MAN her, and away again to sea.
 This is our author's aim;--- and if his art
Waken to sentiment the feeling heart;
If in his scenes alternate passions burn,
And friendship, love, guilt, virtue take their turn;
If innocence oppress'd lie bleeding here,
You'll give --- 'tis all he asks--- one VIRTUOUS TEAR.

---

 * Tacitus Ann. Lib. 12. Sect. 44, to end of 51.

Dramatis Personæ.

PHARASMANES,	Mr. AICKIN.
RHADAMISTUS,	Mr. BARRY.
TERIBAZUS,	Mr. HOLLAND.
ZOPIRON,	Mr. PACKER.
TIGRANES,	Mr. HURST.
MEGISTUS,	Mr. HAVARD.
ZENOBIA,	Mrs. DANCER.
ZELMIRA,	Mrs. BARRY.

Attendants, Guards, &c.

SCENE lies in Pharasmanes' Camp, on the Banks of the Araxes.

ZENOBIA.

ACT the FIRST.

ZELMIRA.

THRO' the wide camp 'tis awful solitude!
On ev'ry tent, which at the morning's dawn
Rung with the din of arms, deep silence sits
Adding new terrors to the dreadful scene!
My heart dies in me!—hark!—with hideous roar
The turbulent Araxes foams along,
And rolls his torrent thro' yon depth of woods!
'Tis terrible to hear!—who's there?—Zopiron!

Enter ZOPIRON.

ZELMIRA.

My lord; my husband!—help me; lend your aid!

ZOPIRON.

Why didst thou leave thy tent?—why thus afflict
Thy anxious breast, thou partner of my heart?
Why wilt thou thus distract thy tender nature
With groundless fears—e're yonder sun shall visit
The western sky, all will be hush'd to peace.

ZELMIRA.

The interval is horrid; big with woe,
With consternation, peril and dismay!
And oh! if here, while yet the fate of nations
Suspended hangs upon the doubtful sword,
If here the trembling heart thus shrink with horror,

Here

Here in these tents, in this unpeopled camp,
Oh! think, Zopiron, in yon field of death
Where numbers soon in purple heaps shall bleed,
What feelings there must throb in ev'ry breast?
How long, ambition, wilt thou stalk the earth
And thus lay waste mankind!———

ZOPIRON.

This day at length
The warlike king, victorious Pharasmanes
Closes the scene of war.—The Roman bands
But ill can cope with the embattled numbers
Asia pours forth, a firm undaunted host!
A nation under arms!—and every bosom
To deeds of glory fir'd!—Iberia then———

ZELMIRA.

Perish Iberia!—may the sons of Rome
Pour rapid vengeance on her falling ranks,
That he, who tramples on the rights of nature,
May see his vassals over-whelm'd in ruin,
May from yon field be led in sullen chains,
To grace the triumph of imperial Rome;
And from th' assembled senate humbly learn
The dictates of humanity and justice!

ZOPIRON.

Thy generous zeal, thy ev'ry sentiment
Charms my delighted soul.—But thou be cautious,
And check the rising ardor that inflames thee.
The tyrant spares nor sex, nor innocence———

ZELMIRA.

Indignant of controul, he spurns each law,
Each holy sanction, that restrains the nations,
And forms 'twixt man and man the bond of peace.

ZOPIRON.

This is the tyger's den; with human gore
For ever floats the pavement; with the shrieks
Of matrons weeping o'er their slaughter'd sons,
The cries of virgins to the brutal arms
Of violation dragg'd, with ceaseless groans

Of

Of varied misery for ever rings
The dreary region of his curs'd domain.

ZELMIRA.

To multiply his crimes, a beauteous captive,
Th' afflicted Ariana—she—for her,
For that fair excellence my bosom bleeds!
She, in the prime of ev'ry blooming grace,
When next the glowing hour of riot comes,
Shall fall a victim to his base desires———

ZOPIRON.

The bounteous gods may succour virtue still!
In this day's battle, which perhaps e're now
The charging hosts have join'd, should Roman valour
Prevail o'er Asia's numbers.———

ZELMIRA.

That event
Is all our hope.—And lo! on yonder rampart
Trembling with wild anxiety she stands,
Invokes each god, and bids her straining eye
Explore the distant field.———

ZOPIRON.

Yes, there she's fix'd
A statue of despair!———That tender bosom
Heaves with no common grief—I've mark'd her oft,
And if I read aright, some mighty cause
Of hoarded anguish, some peculiar woe
Preys on her mind unseen!—But, ha! behold,
She faints;—her fears too pow'rful for her frame
Sink that frail beauty drooping to the earth.
[*Exit hastily.*

ZELMIRA.

Haste, fly, Zopiron, fly with instant succour;
Support her; help her;—Lo! th' attendant train
Have caught her in their arms!—assist her heav'n,
Assuage the sorrows of that gentle spirit!
Her flutt'ring sense returns;—and now this way
The virgins lead her.—May the avenging gods!
In pity of the woes such virtue feels,

In pity of the wrongs a world endures,
With pow'r resistless arm the Roman legions,
That they may hurl in one collected blow
Assur'd destruction on the tyrant's head!———

Enter ZENOBIA, *leaning on two attendants.*

ZENOBIA.

A little onward, still a little onward
Support my steps———

ZELMIRA.

How fares it, madam, now?

ZENOBIA.

My strength returns—I thank ye, gen'rous maids,
And would I could requite you—fruitless thanks
Are all a wretch can give.———

First attendant,

The gentle office
Of mild benevolence our nature prompts———
Your merit too commands:—on Ariana
We tend with willing, with delighted care,
And that delight o'er pays us for our trouble.

ZENOBIA.

Your cares for me denote a heart that feels
For others woes.—Methinks with strength renew'd
I could adventure forth again.———

Second attendant.

'Twere best
Repose your wearied spirits—we will seek
Yon rising ground, and bring the swiftest tidings
Of all the mingled tumult.

ZENOBIA,

Go, my virgins;
Watch well each movement of the marshall'd field;
Each turn of fortune;—let me know it all;———
Each varying circumstance.———

ZENOBIA.

A TRAGEDY.

ZENOBIA, ZELMIRA.

ZELMIRA.

And will you thus,
Be doom'd for ever, Ariana, thus
A willing prey to visionary ills,
The self-consuming votarist of care?

ZENOBIA.

Alas! I'm doom'd to weep—the wrath of heav'n
With inexhausted vengeance follows still,
And each day comes with aggravated woes.

ZELMIRA.

Yet when Iberia's king, when Pharasmanes,
With all a lover's fondness ——

ZENOBIA.

Name him not!
Name not a monster horrible with blood,
The widows, orphans, and the virgin's tears!

ZELMIRA.

Yet savage as he is, at sight of thee
Each fiercer passion softens into love.
To you he bends; the monarch of the east
Dejected droops beneath your cold disdain,
And all the tyranny of female pride.

ZENOBIA.

That pride is virtue;—virtue that abhors
The tyrant reeking from a brother's murder!
Oh! Mithridates! ever honour'd shade!
—— Peaceful he reign'd, dispensing good around him,
In the mild eye of honourable days! ——
Thro' all her peopled realm Armenia felt
His equal sway;—the sunset of his pow'r
With fainter beams, but undiminish'd glory,
Still shone serene, while ev'ry conscious subject
With tears of praise beheld his calm decline,
And bless'd the parting ray!— yet then, Zelmira,
Oh! fact accurs'd!— yes Pharasmanes then,

Detested

Detested perfidy! — nor ties of blood,
Nor sacred laws, nor the just gods restrain him; —
In the dead midnight hour the fell assassin
Rush'd on the slumber of the virtuous man; —
His life blood gush'd; — the venerable king
Wak'd, saw a brother arm'd against his life,
—Forgave him and expir'd!

ZELMIRA.

Yet wherefore open
Afresh the wounds, which time long since hath clos'd?
——This Day confirms his sceptre in his hand.

ZENOBIA.

Confirms his sceptre --- his ! --- indignant gods,
Will no red vengeance from your stores of wrath
Burst down to crush the tyrant in his guilt?
His sceptre, saidst thou? --- urge that word no more ---
The sceptre of his son! --- the solemn right
Of Rhadamistus! --- Mithridates' choice,
That call'd him to his daughter's nuptial bed,
Approv'd him lineal heir; --- consenting nobles,
The public will, the sanction of the laws,
All ratified his claim; — yet curs'd ambition,
Deaf to a nation's voice, a nation's charter,
Nor satisfied to fill Iberia's throne,
Made war, unnatural war, against a son,
Usurp'd his crown, and with remorseless rage
Pursued his life.

ZELMIRA.

Can Ariana plead
For such a son? --- means she to varnish o'er
The guilt of Rhadamistus?

ZENOBIA.

Guilt, Zelmira!

ZELMIRA.

Guilt that shoots horror thro' my aching heart! ---
Poor lost Zenobia!

ZENOBIA,

ZENOBIA.
And do her misfortunes
Awaken tender pity in your breast?

ZELMIRA.
Ill-fated princess! in her vernal bloom
By a false husband murder'd!—from the stem
A Rose-bud torn, and in some desert cave
Thrown by to moulder into silent dust!——

ZENOBIA.
You knew not Rhadamistus!—Pharasmanes
Knew not the early virtues of his son.
As yet an infant, in his tend'rest years
His father sent him to Armenia's court,
That Mithridates' care might form his mind
To arts, to wisdom, and to manners worthy
Armenia's sceptre, and Zenobia's love.
The world delighted saw each dawning virtue,
Each nameless grace to full perfection rising!—
Oh! he was all the fondest maid could wish,
All truth, all honour, tenderness and love!
Yet from his empire thrown! with merciless fury
His father following,—slaughter raging round,
What could the hero in that dire extreme?

ZELMIRA.
Those strong impassion'd looks!—some fatal secret
Works in her heart, and melts her into tears. [*Aside.*

ZENOBIA.
Driv'n to the margin of Araxes' flood,—
No means of flight,—aghast he look'd around,—
Wild throbb'd his bosom with conflicting passions,—
And must I then?— tears gush'd and choak'd his voice,—
—And must I leave thee then Zenobia?—must
Thy beauteous form—he paus'd, then aim'd a poniard
At his great heart—but oh! I rush'd upon him,
And with these arms close-wreathing round his neck,
With all the vehemence of pray'rs and shrieks,
Implor'd the only boon he then could grant
To perish with him in a fond embrace.——
The foe drew near — time press'd, — no way was left—

He

He clasp'd me to his heart---together both,
Lock'd in the folds of love, we plung'd at once,
And saught a requiem in the roaring flood.

ZELMIRA.

---This wondrous tale---this sudden burst of passion---

ZENOBIA.

Ha!—whither has my frenzy led me?—hark!—
That sound of triumph!—lost, for ever lost!
Ruin'd Armenia——oh! devoted race!

A flourish of trumpets.

Enter TIGRANES, Soldiers, *and some* Prisoners.

ZENOBIA.

Thy looks, Tigranes, indicate thy purpose!
The armies met, and Pharasmanes conquer'd;
Is it not so?

TIGRANES.

As yet with pent up fury
The soldier pants to let destruction loose.
With eager speed we urg'd our rapid march,
To where the Romans tented in the vale
With cold delay protract the ling'ring war.
At our approach their scanty numbers form
Their feeble lines, the future prey of vengeance.

ZENOBIA.

And wherefore, when thy sword demands its share
Of havock in that scene of blood and horror,
Wherefore return'st thou to this lonely camp?

TIGRANES.

With cautious eye as I explor'd the forest,
Which rises thick near yonder ridge of mountains,
And stretches o'er th' interminable plain,
I saw these captives in the gloomy wood
Seeking with silent march the Roman camp.
Impal'd alive 'tis Pharasmanes' will
They suffer death in misery of torment.

ZENOBIA.

ZENOBIA.

Unhappy men!—and must they——ha!—that face,
That aged mien!—that venerable form!—
Immortal pow'rs!—is it my more than father?——
—Is that Megistus?——

MEGISTUS.

Ariana here!
Gods! could I ever hope to see her more?
Thou virtuous maid!——thou darling of my age!——

ZENOBIA.

It is—it is Megistus!——once again
Thus let me fall and clasp his rev'rend knee,
Print the warm kiss of gratitude and love
Upon this trembling hand, and pour the tears,
The mingled tears of wonder and of joy.——

MEGISTUS.

Rise, Ariana, rise—allmighty gods!
The tide of joy and transport pours too fast
Along these wither'd veins—it is too much
For a poor weak old man, worn out with grief
And palsied age,—it is too much to bear!
Oh! Ariana,---daughter of affliction,
Have I then found thee?——do I thus behold thee!---
Now I can die content!——

ZENOBIA.

Thou best of men!
These joys our tears and looks can only speak.——

MEGISTUS.

Yet they are cruel joys---mysterious heav'n!
You bid the storm o'ercast our darksome ways;
You gild the cloud with gleams of cheering light;
Then comes a breath from you, and all is vanish'd!

ZENOBIA.

Wherefore dejected thus——

MEGISTUS.

Alas! to meet thee

C But

But for a moment, and then part for ever!
To meet thee here, only to grieve thee more,
To add to thy afflictions,——— wound that bosom
Where mild affection,———— where each virtue dwells,
Just to behold thee, and then close my eyes
In endless night, while you survey my pangs
In the approaching agony of torment————

ZENOBIA.

Talk not of agony;———'tis rapture all!
And who has pow'r to tear thee from my heart?

MEGISTUS.

Alas! the charge of vile imputed guilt————

ZENOBIA.

I know thy truth, thy pure exalted mind————
Thy sense of noble deeds——— imputed guilt————
Oh! none will dare—hast thou Tigranes?———what,
What is his crime?———blush, foul traducer, blush!————
Oh! *(to Megistus)* the wide world must own thy ev'ry virtue.———

TIGRANES.

If in the conscious forest I beheld
Their dark complottings————

ZENOBIA.

Peace, vile sland'rer, peace!————
Thou know'st who captivates a monarch's heart————
'Tis I protect him——— Ariana does it!————
Thou, venerable man! in my pavillion
I'll lodge thee safe from danger——— oh! this joy,
This best supreme delight the gods have sent,
In pity for whole years of countless woe.
       [*Exit with* Megistus.

ZELMIRA, TIGRANES.

TIGRANES.

With what wild fury her conflicting passions
Rise to a storm, a tempest of the soul!
           I know

I know the latent caufe --- her heart revolts,
And leagues in fecret with the Roman arms.

ZELMIRA.

Beware Tigranes !---that excefs of joy,
Thofe quick, thofe varied paffions ftrongly fpeak
The ftranger has an int'reft in her heart.
Befides, thou know'ft o'er Pharafmanes' will
She holds fupreme dominion———

TIGRANES.

True, fhe rules him
With boundlefs fway——

ZELMIRA.

Nay, more to wake thy fears———
The youthful prince, the valiant Teribazus
In fecret fighs, and feels the ray of beauty
Through ev'ry fenfe foft-thrilling to his heart.
He too becomes thy foe. ——

TIGRANES.

Unguarded man!
Whate'er he loves or hates, with gen'rous warmth,
As nature prompts, that dares he to avow,
And lets each paffion ftand confefs'd to view;
Such too is Ariana ; --- bold and open
She kindly gives inftructions to her foe,
To marr her beft defigns.——

ZELMIRA.

Her foe, Tigranes!
That lovely form infhrines the gentleft virtues,
Softeft compaffion, unaffected wifdom,
To outward beauty lending higher charms
Adorning and adorn'd!---The gen'rous prince,——
He too --- full well thou know'ft him --- he unites
In the heroic mould of manly firmnefs,
Each mild attractive art --- oh ! furely none
Envy the fair renown that's earn'd by virtue.

TIGRANES.

None fhould Zelmira!---ha! thofe warlike notes!

Enter

Enter TERIBAZUS.

TERIBAZUS.

Each weary foldier reft upon his arms,
And wait the king's return---Zelmira fay,
In thefe dark moments of impending horror,
How fares thy beauteous friend?---her tender fpirit
But ill fupports the fierce alarms of war.

Enter ZENOBIA.

ZENOBIA.

Where is he?---let me fly---oh! Pharafmanes------
Methought thofe founds befpoke the king's approach------
Oh! Teribazus, tell me---have the fates------
This horrible fufpenfe------

TERIBAZUS.

I came, bright maid,
To hufh the wild emotions of thy heart.
Devouring flaughter for a while fufpends
It's ruthlefs rage;---as either hoft advanc'd
In dread array, and from the burnifh'd arms
Of Afia's ranks redoubled funbeams play'd
Burning with bright diverfities of day,
Came forth an herald from the Roman camp
With proferr'd terms---my father deign'd for once
To yield to mild perfuafion---in his tent
Th' ambaffador of Rome will foon attend him
To fheathe the fword, and give the nations peace.

ZENOBIA.

But oh! no peace for me, misfortune's heir!
The wretched heir of mifery!---But now
A more then father found,---yet cruel men
Would tear him from me---gen'rous, gen'rous prince,
Spare an old man, whofe head is white with age,
Nor let 'em wound me with the fharpeft pang
That ever tortur'd a poor bleeding heart.

TERIBAZUS.

Teribazus.

Arise my fair;—let not a storm of grief
Thus bend to earth my Ariana's beauties;
Soon shall they all revive———

Zenobia.

They brought him fetter'd,
Bound like a murderer!—Tigranes,—he,———
This is the author of the horrid charge———
He threatens instant death—but oh! protect,
Protect an innocent, a good old man,———
Or stretch me with him on the mournful bier.

Teribazus.

By heav'n, whoe'er he is, since dear to you,
He shall not suffer—quick, direct me to him———
My guards shall safe inclose him.

Zenobia.

In my pavillion
He waits his doom———

Teribazus.

Myself will bear the tidings
Of life, of joy, and liberty restor'd.———
And thou artificer of ill, thou false,
Thou vile defamer!—leave thy treach'rous arts,
Nor dare accuse whom Ariana loves.

Zenobia, Zelmira.

Zenobia.

Zelmira,—this is happiness supreme!
Oh! to have met with unexampl'd goodness
To owe my all, my very life itself,
To an unknown but hospitable hand,
And thus enabled by the bounteous gods,
To pay the vast, vast debt———'tis ecstacy

That swells above all bounds, till the fond heart
Ache with delight, and thus run o'er in tears.

ZELMIRA.

What must Zelmira think?——at first your tongue
Grew lavish in the praise of Rhadamistus,
With hints obscure touching your high descent;——
And now this hoary sage——is he your father?
My mind is lost in wonder and in doubt.——

ZENOBIA.

Then to dispel thy doubts, and tell at once
What deep reserve has hid within my heart,
——I am Zenobia—I that ill-starr'd wretch!
The daughter of a scepter'd ancestry,
And now the slave of Mithridates' brother!

ZELMIRA.

Long lost Zenobia, and restor'd at length!
I am your subject; oh! my queen! my sov'reign!

ZENOBIA.

Thou gen'rous friend! rise, my Zelmira, rise.
—That good old man!—oh! it was he beheld me
Borne far away from Rhadamistus' arms,
Just perishing, just lost!——
He dash'd into the flood, redeem'd me thence,
And brought me back to life.—My op'ning eyes
Just saw the light, and clos'd again to shun it.
Each vital pow'r was sunk, but he, well skill'd
In potent herbs, recall'd my flutt'ring soul.

ZELMIRA.

May the propitious gods reward his care.

ZENOBIA.

With me he sav'd a dear, a precious boy,
Then in the womb conceal'd;—he sav'd my child
To trace his father's lov'd resemblance to me,
The dear, dear offspring of our bridal loves.

ZELMIRA.

ZELMIRA.

Oh! bleſſings on him, bleſſings on his head!———

ZENOBIA.

Reſign'd and patient I ſince dwelt with him———
Far in the mazes of a winding wood,
Midſt hoary mountains, and deep cavern'd rocks.
But oh! the fond idea of my lord
Purſued me ſtill, or in the cavern'd rock,
The mountain's brow, and pendent foreſt's gloom.
The ſun look'd joyleſs down;—each lonely night
Heard my griefs ecchoing thro' the woodland ſhade.
—My infant Rhadamiſtus!—he is loſt,
He too is wreſted from me!—'midſt the rage
And the wide waſte of war, the hell-hound troops
Of Pharaſmanes ſought my lone retreat,
And from the violated ſhades, from all
My ſoul held dear, the barb'rous ruffians tore me,
And never ſhall the wretched mother ſee
Her child again!———

ZELMIRA.

Heav'n may reſtore him ſtill,———
May ſtill reſtore your royal huſband too———
Who knows but ſome protecting god———

ZENOBIA.

No god!
No guardian pow'r was preſent!—he is loſt!———
Oh! Rhadamiſtus!—oh! my honour'd lord!
No pitying eye beheld thy decent form;———
The rolling flood devour'd thee!———thou haſt found
A watry grave, and the laſt diſmal accents
That trembled on thy tongue, came bubbling up,
And murmur'd loſt Zenobia!

ZELMIRA.

Yet be calm.———
The gods may bring redreſs—even now they give
To miſery like thine, the heartfelt joy
Of ſhielding injured virtue.

ZENOBIA.

ZENOBIA.

Yes, Zelmira,
That pure delight is mine, a ray from heav'n
That bids affliction smile—All gracious pow'rs!
Make me your agent here to save Megistus,
I'll bear the load of life,—bear all its ills
Till you shall bid this sad world-weary spirit
    To peaceful regions wing her happy flight,
  And seek my lord in the dark realms of night;
  Seek his dear shade in ev'ry pensive grove,
  And bear him all my constancy and love.

END OF THE FIRST ACT.

ACT the SECOND.

TIGRANES.

A False accuser deem'd!---artificer of fraud!
Those words, intemp'rate boy---thy phrenzy too
Deluded fair!---shall cost you dear attonement.
Yet till occasion rise--- the king approaches.
　　　　　　　　　　　[Grand warlike music.

A Military Procession: Enter Pharasmanes, *&c.*

PHARASMANES.

At length the fame of Pharasmanes' arms
Hath aw'd the nations round——Rome shrinks aghast
With pale dismay, recalls her trembling legions,
And deprecates the war——oh! what a scene
Of glorious havoc had yon field beheld,
If peaceful counsels had not check'd my fury!
——Valiant Tigranes, those rebellious slaves,
Thy care detected— have they suffer'd death?

TIGRANES.

Your pardon, Sir— their doom as yet suspended——
The gen'rous prince—I would not utter aught
Should injure Teribazus——

PHARASMANES.

Ha!— proceed,
And give me all the truth——

TIGRANES.

By his command —
His tender nature deem'd it barb'rous rigour
To urge their sentence —

PHARASMANES.

Vain aspiring boy!
Tell Teribazus,　　[*Enter* Zenobia]
　　　　　——tell th' unthinking prince,
　　　　　　　　D　　　　　　　　　　　The

The rash presumptuous stripling, these his arts,
These practices of popular demeanour,
Are treason to his father — let him know
Thro' wide Armenia and Iberia's realm
My will is fate — the slaves shall meet their doom.

ZENOBIA.

Oh! mighty king, — thus bending lowly down, ——
An humble suppliant ———

PHARASMANES.

Ariana here!
Thou beauteous mourner, let no care molest
Thy tender bosom; — rise and bid thy charms
Beam forth thy gentlest lustre to adorn
The glories of my triumph.

ZENOBIA.

Oh! a wretch like me
It best befits thus groveling on the earth
To bathe your feet with tears ———

PHARASMANES.

It must not be ——— [*He raises her.*
By heav'n renown in arms in vain attends me,
If the lov'd graces of thy matchless form
Are thus depress'd and languish in affliction,
Like flow'rs that droop and hang their pining heads
Beneath the rigour of relentless skies,

ZENOBIA.

If thou would'st raise me from the depths of woe,
Forgive those captives, whom thy fatal anger
Adjudg'd to death, nor let ill-tim'd resentment
Fall on the prince your son — 'twas I — my tears ——
My piercing lamentations won his heart
To arrest their doom ———

PHARASMANES.

For traitors to my crown
Does Ariana plead? ———

ZENOBIA.

A TRAGEDY.

ZENOBIA.

For mild humanity
My suppliant voice is rais'd — I point the means
To add new glory to your fame in arms.
In naught so near can men approach the gods
As the dear act of giving life to others.———
In feats of war the glory is divided,
To all imparted,— to each common man,———
And fortune too shall vindicate her share.———
— But of sweet mercy,—the vast, vast renown
Is all your own; nor officer, nor soldier
Can claim a part — the praise, the honour'd praise,
Adorns the victor, — nor is th' eccho lost
'Midst shouts of armies, and the trumpet's sound.
He conquers even victory itself,
Than hero more — a blessing to the world!———

PHARASMANES.

Thy eloquence disarms my stubborn soul.
But wherefore urgent thus?—amidst the band
Is there who claims thy soft solicitude?

ZENOBIA.

A hoary sage — alas! a more than father———
The best of men — preserver of my being,———
A blameless shepherd!— rude of fraud and guilt,
Innoxious thro' his life— oh! mighty king,
Spare an old man,— a venerable sire!
Naught has your fortune greater than the pow'r
To serve humanity!— shew that your heart
Has the sweet grace, the gen'rous virtue too!

PHARASMANES.

My soul relents, and yields to thy entreaty,
Thy violence of pray'r — release him streight———
My brightest honours wait him;— honours fit
For him who gave thee birth;— for him whose virtue
Thy gen'rous soul deems worthy its esteem.

ZENOBIA.

Our humble station seeks nor pomp nor splendor———
We only ask, unenvied and obscure,
To live in blameless innocence,— to seek

Our calm retreat, embrac'd in depth of woods,
And dwell with peace and humble virtue there.

PHARASMANES.

That cold disdain, which shuns admiring eyes,
Attracts the more, exalting ev'ry charm.
No more of humble birth — thy matchless beauty,
Like gems, that in the mine conceal their lustre,
Was form'd to dignify the eastern throne.
My scepter, that strikes terror to each heart,
Grac'd by thy decent hand shall make each subject
Adore thy softer sway — The glorious æra
Of Pharasmanes' love, — his date of empire
With Ariana shar'd, henceforth begins,
And leads the laughing hours — but first the storm
Of war and wild commotion must be hush'd ———
That mighty care now calls me to my throne,
To give the Roman audience; audience fit
To strike a citizen of Rome with awe,
When he beholds the majesty of kings. [*going*.

Enter TERIBAZUS.

TERIBAZUS.

Dread Sir, the Roman embassy approaches.———
From yonder rampart, that invests your camp,
I heard their horses hoofs with eager speed
Beat the resounding soil.———

PHARASMANES.

Let 'em approach———
And thou, whose arrogance — but I forbear———
When Ariana pardons, my resentment
Yields to her smiles, and looks away its rage.
As when the crimes of men Jove's wrath demand,
And the red thunder quivers in his hand;
The queen of love his vengeance can disarm
With the soft eloquence of ev'ry charm;
Controul his passions with resistless sway,
And the impending storm smile to serenest day.
[*Exit with his train.*

ZENOBIA.

A TRAGEDY.

ZENOBIA, TERIBAZUS.

TERIBAZUS.

And may I then once more, thou bright perfection,
May Teribazus once again approach thee,
While thus my father,—my ambitious father,
At sight of thee forgets his cruel nature,
And wonders how he feels thy beauty's pow'r?
Oh! may I—but I'm too importunate——
Your looks rebuke me from you,—and I see
How hateful I am grown!——

ZENOBIA.

Mistake me not
Nor rashly thus arraign the looks of one,
Whose heart lies bleeding here—thy gen'rous worth
Is oft the live-long day my fav'rite theme.
But oh! for me,—for wretched Ariana,
The god of love long since hath quench'd his torch,
And ev'ry source of joy lies dead within me.

TERIBAZUS.

That cold averted look!—but I am us'd
To bear your scorn;—your scorn that wounds the deeper,
Mask'd as it is with pity and esteem.
Yet love incurable,—relentless love
Burns here a constant flame, that rises still,
And will to madness kindle, should I see
That hoard of sweets, that treasury of charms
Yield to another, to a barb'rous rival
Who persecutes a son to his undoing.

ZENOBIA.

If Ariana's happiness would wound thee,
Thou'lt ne'er have cause to murmur or repine.
Naught can divorce me from the black despair
To which I've long been wedded.——

TERIBAZUS.

Calm disdain,
I grant you, well becomes the tyrant fair
Whom Pharasmanes destines for his throne.
But oh! in pity to this breaking heart,

Give

Give me, in mercy give some other rival,
Whom I may stab,—without remorse may stab,
'Midst his delight, in all his heav'n of bliss,
And spurn him from the joys, that scorpion-like
Shoot anguish here—here thro' my very soul.

ZENOBIA.

Alas! too gen'rous prince, the gods long since
Between us both fix'd their eternal bar.

TERIBAZUS.

What say'st thou Ariana?—ha! beware,
Nor urge me to destraction—love like mine,
Fierce, gen'rous, wild,—with disappointment wild,
May rouse my desp'rate rage to do a deed
Will make all nature shudder.—Love despis'd
Not always can respect the ties of nature!————
—Driven to extremes the tend'rest passion scorn'd
May hate at length the object it adores,
And stung to madness—no!—inhuman fair,
You still must be,—in all vicissitudes,
In all the scenes misfortune has in store,
You still must be the sov'reign of my soul.
But for the favour'd, for the happy rival,
By heav'n, whoe'er he be,—despair and phrenzy
May strike the blow, and dash him from your arms
A sacrifice to violated love.

ZENOBIA.

Why thus distract yourself with vain suspicions?
—You have no rival, whom your rage can murder——
—None in the pow'r of fate—oh! Teribazus,
The wretched Ariana—long, long since——
—My heart sweels o'er—I cannot speak—a duty,
A rigorous duty bids me ne'er accept
Thy proferr'd love;—a duty, which, if known,
Would in eternal silence seal thy vows,
Turn all thy rage to tears, and, oh! my prince!
Bid thee respect calamities like mine. [*Exit.*

TERIBAZUS.

Yet Ariana stay—turn, turn and hear me——
She's gone, the cruel, unrelenting fair!

And

And leaves me thus to misery of soul.

Enter ZOPIRON.

Flamminius, from the Romans is arriv'd,
And bears the olive-branch—the king your father
Assembles all his nobles——

TERIBAZUS.

Say, Zopiron,
Does Rome yield up Armenia?

ZOPIRON.

Rome is still
The scourge of lawless pow'r—a people's rights
The conscript fathers have resolv'd to shield,
And to the lineal heir assert the crown.

TERIBAZUS.

May the stern god of battles aid their arms,
And fight with the deliverers of mankind!
Unnatural father! that would seize my scepter,
Mine as my brother's heir, and ravish with it
The idol of my soul—but now no more
His tyranny prevails—to empire rais'd,
'Twill be the pride of my exulting heart,
To lay my crown at Ariana's feet.   [*Exit.*

ZOPIRON.

Unhappy prince! should Pharasmanes know
His ardent passion for the captive maid,
Alas! his fatal rage—propitious pow'rs!
May these events,—may Rome's ambassador,——
Oh! may he come with concord in his train,
And far avert the ills my heart forebodes!——
But lo! Flamminius.——

Enter RHADAMISTUS.

ZOPIRON.

Welcome to these tents
The harbinger of peace!

RHADAMISTUS.

Does your king know
Flamminius waits his leisure?

ZOPIRON.

ZOPIRON.

He prepares
To hear you, Roman!——

RHADAMISTUS.

As I tread his camp
There is I know not what of horror shoots
Thro' all my frame, and disconcerted reason
Suspends her function,—a black train of crimes,
Murders, and lust, and rapine, cities sack'd,
Nations laid waste by the destructive sword,
A thousand ruthless deeds all rise to view,
And shake my inmost soul, as I approach
The author of calamity and ruin.

ZOPIRON.

Then from a Roman, from a son of freedom
Let the fell tyrant hear the voice of truth,
The strong resistless strain, which liberty
Breathes in her capitol, till his proud heart
Shudder with inward horror at itself.

RHADAMISTUS.

In Pharasmanes' camp that honest stile!——
—Thy visage bears the characters of virtue.——
—Wilt thou impart thy name and quality?

ZOPIRON.

In me you see Zopiron!—deem me not
A vile abettor of the tyrant's guilt.————
To me Armenia trusts her sacred rights;
Hither her chosen deligate she sends me,
At the tribunal of Iberia's king,
To plead her cause, an injur'd people's cause!
Oh! never, never shall my native land
Yield to a vile usurper.

RHADAMISTUS.

Rome has heard
Thy patriot toil for freedom—Rhadamistus
Has heard thy gen'rous ardor in his cause,
And pants to recompence thy truth and zeal.

ZOPIRON.

A TRAGEDY.

ZOPIRON.

Oh! name not Rhadamistus—now no more
The god-like youth shall bless Armenia's realm.
The fates just shew'd him to the wond'ring world,
And then untimely snatch'd him from our sight!—

RHADAMISTUS.

And didst thou know the prince?

ZOPIRON.

My lot severe
Denied that transport;—but the voice of fame
Endears his memory.

RHADAMISTUS.

A time may come
When you may meet, and both in friendship burn.
——Still Rhadamistus lives!———

ZOPIRON.

Said'st thou Flamminius!———
Lives he?

RHADAMISTUS.

Still he survives;—from death and peril
Sav'd by a miracle!—and now for him
Rome claims Armenia.———

ZOPIRON.

Claims Armenia for him!———
For Rhadamistus claims!—and will ye, gods!
Still will ye give him to a nation's pray'rs?

RHADAMISTUS.

Alas! he lives;—heart-broken, desolate,
In sorrow plung'd,—abandon'd to despair!———

ZOPIRON.

The righteous gods will vindicate his cause.———
His lov'd Zenobia, Mithridates' daughter,
That ev'ry excellence—does she too live?

E   Have

Have the indulgent pow'rs watch'd o'er her fate,
And sav'd her for her people?———

RHADAMISTUS.

There, Zopiron,
There lies the wound that pierces to his soul,
The sharpest pang,—that rends—that cleaves his heart.
—Oh! never more shall lovely lost Zenobia,
That angel form, that pattern of all goodness,
No, never more—she's gone, for ever gone!———
Thou would'st not think—her barb'rous, cruel husband—
With his own hand—the recollected tale
Of horror shakes my frame to dissolution!———
Her husband!—he!—that dear, that tender form—
Oh!—poor Zenobia—oh!— [*Falls into a swoon.*

ZOPIRON.

He faints;—he falls!———
Can Roman stoicism thus dissolve
In tender pity?—rise, Flamminius, rise;
He stirs; he breathes;—and life begins to wander
O'er his forsaken cheek.—Resume thy strength,
And like a Roman triumph o'er your tears.———

RHADAMISTUS.

I'll not be forc'd back to a wretched world.———
No;—let me,—let me die.———

ZOPIRON.

His eyes reject
The cheerful light—what can this anguish mean?

RHADAMISTUS.

You do but waste your pains;—it is in vain!—
Away and leave a murd'rer to his woes.———

ZOPIRON.

Why thus accuse thyself?—I'll not believe it—
Thus let me raise thee from the earth ———

RHADAMISTUS.

Alas! (*rising*)———
Despair weighs heavy on me.

ZOPIRON.

ZOPIRON.

Still I muſt
Controul this ſudden phrenzy——

RHADAMISTUS.

Oh!—Zopiron,
Here,—here it lies——

ZOPIRON.

Unburthen all, and eaſe
Your loaded heart—it cannot be—thou never wert
A murd'rer!——

RHADAMISTUS.

Yes!—the horror of the world!——
A murd'rous wretch!—the fatal Rhadamiſtus!——
'Twas I—theſe felon hands!—with treach'rous love
I claſp'd her in this curs'd embrace—I bore her
In theſe deteſted arms, and gave that beauty,
That tender form to the devouring waves.——
Plunge me, ye furies, in your lakes of fire——
Here fix,—fix all your vultures in my heart!——
And lo! they ruſh upon me *(ſtarts up)* ſee! ſee there!
With racks and wheels they come;--they tear me piece-meal--
'Tis juſt Zenobia!——I deſerve it all——
[*Falls upon* Zopiron.

ZOPIRON.

Aſſiſt him guardian pow'rs!—your own high will
Guides theſe events!—revive, my prince, revive!

RHADAMISTUS.

Why thus recall me to deſpair and horror?
To bid me hate the light, deteſt myſelf,
Traitor to nature,—traitor to my love!——
—And yet, Zopiron,—yet I am not plung'd
So far in guilt, but thou may'ſt pity me!——
Heav'n, I atteſt,—yes you can witneſs gods!
I meant to periſh with her—but the fates
Denied that comfort---from her circling arms
The torrent bore me far---expiring, ſenſeleſs,
Gaſping in death, the overflowing tide

Impetuous

Impetuous drove me on th' unwish'd for shore.
—There soon deserted by the merciless stream
A band of Romans, as from Syria's frontier
They rang'd the country round,---descried me stretch'd
Pale and inanimate---with barb'rous pity
They lent their aid, and chain'd me to the rack
Of inauspicious life!———

ZOPIRON.

For wond'rous ends
Mysterious providence has still reserv'd you,
To circulate the happiness of millions,
A patriot prince———

RHADAMISTUS.

Would they had let me perish!———
What has a wretch like me to do in life,
When my Zenobia's lost?---'tis true, my friend,
She begg'd to die---but that pathetic look,
Her tears, embraces, and those streaming eyes
Still beauteous in distress!---each winning grace,
Her ev'ry charm should have forbid the deed,
And pleaded for her life!

ZOPIRON.

And yet, my prince,
When self-acquitting conscience———

RHADAMISTUS.

Self-condemn'd
My soul is rack'd,---is tortur'd---not her child,
Her unborn infant,---the first fruit of love,
Not ev'n her babe could with the voice of nature
Plead for itself,---or for its wretched mother.———
They perish'd both,---she and her little one,
And I survive to tell it.———

ZOPIRON.

Let not grief
O'erwhelm your reason thus---what! when your father,
Your cruel father, recking from the blood
Of Mithridates---

RHADAMISTUS.

RHADAMISTUS.

Naught but death was left,
Yet ev'n that laſt, ſad refuge was debarr'd me!——
E'er ſince I've liv'd in miſery;—my days
Were colour'd all with anguiſh and deſpair!
Long from the Romans I conceal'd my name.
At length reveal'd me to a choſen friend;——
—Journey'd with him to Rome; and in full ſenate
Told all the diſmal ſtory of my woes.
The conſcript fathers heard, and dropt a tear——
Then to quick vengeance fir'd, diſpatch'd their legions
To wage the war; Paulinus leads them on,
And now to me commits this embaſſy,
With fully delegated pow'rs from Rome.

ZOPIRON.

With one united voice Armenia calls
For Mithridates' heir!—convinc'd by rumour
That thou ar't loſt, the gen'ral cry demands
Your brother Teribazus——

RHADAMISTUS.

He, Zopiron,
Is to theſe eyes a ſtranger.——

ZOPIRON.

Hapleſs prince!
A cloud of woes lies brooding o'er his head.
A fair, a lovely captive rules his heart;
Her name is Ariana; and indeed
No wonder ſhe attracts his ſoft regard,
And kindles all the vehemence of love.
The tyrant eyes her too with fierce deſire,——
And ruin nods o'er Teribazus' head.

RHADAMISTUS.

By heav'n it ſhall not be—alas! I know
The pang of loſing whom the heart adores. ——
I'll yield him up Armenia—what are crowns
But toys of vain ambition, when the lov'd
The dear pertaker of my throne is loſt?

Enter TIGRANES.

ZOPIRON.

What would Tigranes?

TIGRANES.

Pharasmanes calls
Flamminius to his presence ———

RHADAMISTUS.

I attend him;———
So tell your king———

TIGRANES.

Instant he waits thee Roman.   [*Exit.*

RHADAMISTUS.

How my heart trembles at the awful meeting!

ZOPIRON.

Then summon all your strength—the lapse of time
From early youth, when Pharasmanes saw you,
Affliction's inward stroke,—that Roman garb,
All will protect, and cloak you from detection!———

RHADAMISTUS.

Zopiron yes; in this important crisis,
When violated laws, and injur'd men,
When my own wrongs are lab'ring in my heart,
The great occasion calls for firmest vigour.
Yes, in this interview I will maintain
A Roman's part;—in Pharasmanes' soul
I'll wake the furies of detested guilt,
And pour the rapid energy of truth
Till ev'n to himself his crimes are known,
And the usurper tremble on his throne.

END OF THE SECOND ACT.

A TRAGEDY.

ACT the THIRD.

PHARASMANES, *on his Throne:* TIGRANES, ZOPIRON, Officers, &c.

PHARASMANES.

WHERE is this bold republican from Rome?
This enemy of kings?—Tigranes, thou
Bid the plebeian enter---Pharasmanes
Vouchsafes him audience.——

Enter FLAMMINIUS.

PHARASMANES.

Now, Flamminius, say
What motive brings you to Araxes' banks,
To wage this slow, this philosophic war?

RHADAMISTUS.

By me, unworthy of th' important charge,
By me, unequal to the arduous theme,
The conscript fathers here explain their conduct,
And justify the ways of Rome to kings.

PHARASMANES.

Roman, thou may'st declaim with all thy pomp
Of idle eloquence.

RHADAMISTUS.

No pow'r of words,
No graceful periods of harmonious speech
Dwell on my lip—the only art I boast
Is honest truth, unpolish'd, unadorn'd!——
Truth that must strike conviction to your heart,
Truth that informs you,---to usurp a crown,
For dire ambition to unpeople realms,
Are violations of each sacred law,
And bid the Roman eagle wing'd with vengeance
To the Araxes' margin bend her flight,
To tell destruction it shall rage no more.

PHARASMANES.

PHARASMANES.

And dares Paulinus' foldier,—dar'ſt thou flave
Thus offer vile indignity, and mouthe
The language of your forum to a king?

RHADAMISTUS.

Rome knows, and owns you as Iberia's king,
But not Armenia's.———

PHARASMANES.

Ha!———

RHADAMISTUS.

Th' aſſembled ſenate
Acknowledges your vaſt renown in arms,
And honours the unſhaken fortitude
Ev'n of a foe—but, Sir, the fortitude,
Whoſe brutal rage lays nations deſolate,
It is the glory of imperial Rome
To humble and ſubdue—it is the glory
Of Rome, that ſpares the vanquiſh'd, 'tis her pride
To ſet the nations free;—to fix the bounds
Of the fell tyrant's pow'r;—to trace the circle
From which he muſt not move—theſe are the arts
The bright prerogative of Rome—of Rome,
The miſtreſs of the world, whoſe conqu'ring banners
O'er Aſia's realms ſo oft have wav'd in triumph,
And made ev'n kings her ſubjects———

PHARASMANES.

Ha! vain boaſter!

RHADAMISTUS.

Made oriental kings, ſhort by the knee
Accept their crown, with tears of joy accept it,
And be the viceroys of a Roman ſenate.

PHARASMANES.

And this to Pharaſmanes?—has not yet
A train of conqueſts taught you to revere
This good right arm in war?—This arm the Parthians
Have felt with fatal overthrow—no ſpoil,

No trophies won from me have grac'd their triumphs;
No friends of mine were harnefs'd to their chariots;—
No captive chief, like your own mangled Craffus,
There roams a fullen ghoft, and calls for vengeance,
For vengeance ftill unpaid, and calls in vain
For the fad funeral rites.—Would Rome prefume
To wreft Armenia from me,—lo! my banners
From frofty Caucafus to Phafis' banks
Wave high in air, and fhadow all the land.
Call your embattled legions—or does Rome,
All conqu'ring Rome, that miftrefs of the world,
Does fhe at length by her ambaffadors
Negotiate thus the war?

RHADAMISTUS.

Rome, Sir, commands
The fubject world, for fhe adores the gods———
And their all-pow'rful aid.———

PHARASMANES.

Would'ft thou difpute
My lawful claim,—arm thee with fword and fire,
Not with vain fubtleties, and idle maxims. ———
Armenia's crown is mine,—deriv'd to me,
Heir to a brother, and a fon deceas'd.———

RHADAMISTUS.

And can a murd'rer, can the midnight ruffian
Prove himfelf heir—by the affaffin's ftab?———

PHARASMANES.

Thou bafe reviler!— [*Comes forward and draws his faber.*

TIGRANES.

Moderate your fury; [*holding him*]
It were unjuft—

ZOPIRON.

The character he bears, ———
The laws of nations ———

PHARASMANES.

Thou bafe infolent!

F

Who

Who dar'st to wound the ear of sacred kings
With a black crime, that's horrible to nature!——

   RHADAMISTUS.

Yes horrible to nature!—yet the world
Has heard it all—thou art the man of blood!
A brother's blood yet smokes upon thy hand—
Not his white age, his venerable looks,
Not ev'n his godlike virtues could withhold thee!—
Gash'd o'er with wounds he falls;—he bleeds, he dies,
Without a groan he dies!—that is thy work,
Thine, murd'rer, thine!——

   PHARASMANES.

No more—the hand of heav'n
Shook from the blasted tree the wither'd fruit——

   RHADAMISTUS.

Forbear the impious strain—it is the stile
Ambition speaks, when for a crown it stabs,
Then dares, with execrable mock'ry dares,
Traduce the governing all-righteous mind.

   PHARASMANES.

He harrows up my soul!—and do'st thou think
A madman's ravings——

   RHADAMISTUS.

Since that hour accurst
Hast thou not plung'd thee deeper still in guilt?
Your son—your blameless son——

   PHARASMANES.

His crimes provok'd
A father's wrath—his and Zenobia's crimes!——

   RHADAMISTUS.

She too—untimely lost—unbidden tears
Forbear to stream, nor quite unman me thus.

   PHARASMANES.

In tears!—by heav'n, thou woman-hearted slave,

            Those

A TRAGEDY.

Those coward symptoms have some latent spring
That lies conceal'd within that treach'rous heart.

RHADAMISTUS.

They are the tears humanity lets fall
When soft ey'd beauty dies untimely slain.——
But to avenge her death, array'd in terror
The Roman legions———

PHARASMANES.

Lead 'em to the charge.——
Thou quit my camp:—If when yon sun descends
Thou linger'st here, the title of ambassador
Shall naught avail to save thee from my fury.

RHADAMISTUS.

E'er that resign Armenia—Till the close
Of day, I give thee leisure to revolve
The vengeance Rome prepares—Thou know'st
With what a pond'rous arm her hardy sons
Lift the avenging spear.—Be timely wise,
Nor dare provoke your fate.   [*Exit.*

PHARASMANES.

Roman farewel!——
Do thou, Tigranes, issue forth my orders
From tent to tent, that each man stand prepar'd
For the dead midnight hour—with silent march
Then will I pour with ruinous assault
Upon th' astonish'd foe, my horses hoofs
Imbrue in blood, and give to-morrow's sun
A spectacle of horror and destruction.——
    [*He ascends his throne, and the back scene closes.*

Enter ZENOBIA *and* MEGISTUS.

ZENOBIA.

Oh! tell me all Megistus; let me hear
All that concerns my child,—my blooming boy,
My little Rhadamistus—is he safe?
Give me the truth—do not deceive a mother
Who doats upon her babe—is my child safe?

MEGISTUS.

Dry up your tears—I cannot bear to see you
Afflicted thus—your infant hero's safe——
You may believe your faithful old Megistus——

ZENOBIA.

I do believe thee—but excuse my weakness——
My flutt'ring fears for ever paint him to me
By ruffians seiz'd, and as he sees the knife
Aim'd at his little throat, in vain imploring
For me by name, and begging my assistance,
While far, far off his miserable mother
No aid can give, nor snatch him to her heart,

MEGISTUS.

I never yet deceiv'd you—by yon heav'n
The prince still lives—when I regain'd my cottage
After the toils of many a weary day,
I found him there—but griev'd and wond'ring much
Where his dear mother was.

ZENOBIA.

Megistus tell me,
Oh! tell me each particular; his looks,
All his apt questions, his enchanting words;
For I could hear of him for ever—lovely youth!
His father's image blooming in his boy!
Thro' sev'n revolving years my only comfort!——
—When from my eyes the sudden sorrows gush'd,
How would he look, and ask his wretched mother
What meant those falling tears?—alas! ev'n now
I see him here before me—did my child
Think his poor mother lost?

MEGISTUS.

At first he seem'd
To pine in thought at your long weary absence,
And many a look he cast, that plainly spoke
His little bosom heav'd with various passions.
Still would he seek you in each well known haunt,
Each bow'r, each cavern, like the tender fawn
That thro' the woodland seeks its mother lost,

Exploring

A TRAGEDY.

Exploring all around with anxious eye,
And looking still unutterable grief,
Lonely and sad, and stung with keen regret.

ZENOBIA.

Did my child weep?—not much I hope——

MEGISTUS.

With soothing tales
I labour'd to beguile him from his sorrow;—
I promis'd your return; a gentle smile
Brighten'd his anxious look; he sigh'd content,
And then I led him to a safer dwelling
Among the shepherds of the Syrain vale,
Who all have sworn to guard him as their own,
And in due season lead him to the Romans.

ZENOBIA.

Oh! may those shepherds know the kindest influence
Of the indulgent heav'ns!—yet why not stay
To guard him—but i'll not complain—on me
Your cares were fix'd—oh! tell me how the gods
Watch'd ov'r all thy ways, and brought thee to me?
Where hast thou liv'd these many, many days?——

MEGISTUS.

In bitterness of soul I've liv'd, thy fate
Thy tender form deep imag'd in my breast!
I rang'd the banks where the Arazes flows,
But bring, alas! no tidings of your lord.
Heart-broken, wearied out, I measur'd back
My feeble steps,—but thou wer't ravish'd thence;——
For thee I travers'd hills and forests drear;
Thee I invok'd, that ev'ry cavern'd rock,
Each vale, each mountain eccho'd with thy name.

ZENOBIA.

And here at length you find me, here encompas'd
With all the worst of ills—hence let us fly
To the bless'd Syrian vally, where my child
Wins with his early manhood ev'ry heart,
And calls for me, and chides this long delay.

MEGISTUS.

MEGISTUS.

Vain the attempt——one only way is left—
Reveal thee to th' ambaſſador of Rome.——
Safe in his train thou may'ſt eſcape this place,
And gain Paulinus' camp—Zenobia known
Will meet protection there.——

ZENOBIA.

The gods inſpire
The happy counſel—ha!—Tigranes comes!
Retire Megiſtus *(he goes out)* a gay dawn of hope
Beams forth at length, and lights up day within me.

ZENOBIA, TIGRANES.

TIGRANES.

Hail princeſs, deſtin'd to imperial ſway,
To grace with beauty Pharaſmanes' throne!
By me the impatient king requeſts you'll fix
The happy nuptial hour.——

ZENOBIA.

Thou might'ſt as well
Command me wed the forked lightnings blaze
That gilds the ſtorm, and be in love with horror.

TIGRANES.

Take heed, raſh fair!—an eaſtern monarch's love,
Ardent as his, muſt not be made the ſport
Of tyrant beauty—when a rival dares
Oppoſe his ſov'reign's wiſh———

ZENOBIA.

Does Pharaſmanes,
Say,—does your king permit his ſpies of ſtate,
That curſe of human kind, to breathe their whiſpers
In his deluded ear?

TIGRANES.

Full well 'tis know
That Teribazus bids you thus revolt,
And draws your heart's allegiance from your king.

ZENOBIA.

ZENOBIA.

Thou vile accuser!——if the prince's virtues
Have touch'd my bosom, what hast thou to urge?
—What if a former Hymeneal vow
Has bound my soul?—what if a father, Sir,
A father dear as my heart's purple drops,
Enjoin a rigid duty ne'er to share
The throne of Mithridates with a murderer?

TIGRANES.

Madam, those words——

ZENOBIA.

Thou instrument of ill!
Who still ar't ready with a tale suborn'd,
And if thou ar't not perjur'd, dar'st betray;—
Away——and let thy conscience tell the rest.   [*Exit.*

TIGRANES, *alone.*

Vain haughty fair!—thou hast provok'd my rage
By wrongs unnumber'd—but for all those wrongs
Soon shall inevitable ruin seize thee.——

Enter RHADAMISTUS.

RHADAMISTUS.

Perhaps e're this your king's tumultuous passions
Sink to a calm, and reason takes her turn.
Then seek him, Sir, and bear a Roman's message,
The terms of peace humanity suggests.
Tell him Flamminius wishes to prevent
The rage of slaughter, and the streams of blood
Which else shall deluge yonder crimson plains.

TIGRANES.

Already, Roman, his resolve is fix'd.——
War, horrid war impends.—

RHADAMISTUS.

And yet in pity
To human kind, to the unhappy millions

Who soon shall die, and with their scatter'd bones
Whiten the plains of Asia,—it were best
To sheathe the sword, and join in Rome's alliance.
Wilt thou convey my message?

TIGRANES.

I obey.——— [*Exit.*

RHADAMISTUS, *alone.*

May some propitious pow'r inspire his heart,
And touch the springs of human kindness in him,
Else against whom amidst the charging hosts
Must Rhadamistus' sword be levell'd?—ha!—
Spite of his crimes he is my father still———
And must this arm against the source of life—
Nay more,—perhaps against a brother too,
---A brother still unknown!---he too may die
By this unconscious hand!---this hand already
Inur'd to murder whom my heart adores!---
---My brother then may bleed!---and when in death
Gasping he lies, and pours his vital stream,
Then in that moment shall the gen'rous youth
Extend his arms, and with a piteous look
Tell me---a brother doth forgive his murderer?---
---Gods! you have doom'd me to the blackest woe,
To be a wretch abhorr'd, author of crimes
From which my tortur'd breast revolts with horror!—
---Who's there?--- a youth comes forward---now be firm,
Be firm my heart, and guard thy fatal secret!---

Enter TERIBAZUS.

TERIBAZUS.

Illustrious Roman,---if misfortune's son
A wretched,———ruin'd———miserable prince
May claim attention----

RHADAMISTUS.

Ha!---can this be he!
The graces of his youth,---each feeling here,
Here at my heartstrings tell me 'tis my brother! [*aside.*

TERIBAZUS.

TERIBAZUS.

I see you're mov'd, and I intrude too far.—

RHADAMISTUS.

Purfue your purpofe—warmeſt friendſhip for you
Glows in this breaſt——

TERIBAZUS.

Tho' Pharaſmanes' fury
Maintains a fix'd hoſtility with Rome,
Blend not the fon with all a father's crimes.——

RHADAMISTUS.

Go on—I pant to hear—

TERIBAZUS.

My father's cruelty
Each day breaks out in fome new act of horror,
Nor lets the fword grow cool from human blood.
Firſt in his brother's breaſt he plung'd it;—then
Inflam'd to fiercer rage 'gainſt his own fon,
Oh! Rhadamiſtus! thou much injur'd prince!—

RHADAMISTUS.

And didſt thou love that brother?

TERIBAZUS.

Gen'rous Roman,
He liv'd far hence remote—I ne'er beheld him,
But the wide world refounded with his fame.

RHADAMISTUS.

Hold, hold my tears!—oh! they will burſt their way
At this his virtuous tenderneſs and love!   [*aſide.*

TERIBAZUS.

And doſt thou weep too Roman?

RHADAMISTUS.

From fuch horror,

And so much cruelty my nature shrinks.——
——Whatever purpose rolls within thy breast,
Boldly confide it—shall I arm'd with vengeance
Assault the purple tyrant in his camp?
Or wilt thou join my steps;—then in the front
Of a brave vet'ran legion head the war,
Seek the usurper 'midst his plumed troops,
And thus avenge mankind?

TERIBAZUS.

No; far from me,
Far be the guilt of meditating aught
Against the life from whence my being sprung.
Let him oppress me,—he's a parent still!——

RHADAMISTUS.

He rives my heart!—oh! what a lot is mine! [aside.

TERIBAZUS.

Not for myself I fear; but oh! Flamminius,
A lovely captive,—'tis for her I tremble;—
For Ariana,—for that sweet perfection;—
She is her sex's boast!—her gentle bosom
Fraught with each excellence!—her form and feature
Touch'd by the hand of elegance;—adorn'd
By ev'ry grace, and cast in beauty's mould!—
—Her Pharasmanes means to ravish from me.—
But thou convey her hence—'tis all I ask.——

RHADAMISTUS.

By heav'n I will—do thou too join our flight;
—Armenia shall be thine, and that sweet maid
Reward thy goodness with connubial love,
Adorn thy throne, and make a nation bless'd!——

TERIBAZUS.

Make Ariana happy;—bear her hence
And save those bright unviolated charms
From Pharasmanes' pow'r—when wish'd for peace
Settles a jarring world, Flamminius then,
Then will I seek thee.—Wilt thou then resign her?

RHADAMISTUS.

RHADAMISTUS.

Yes then, as pure as the unsullied snow
That never felt a sunbeam;---then I'll give her
Back to thy faithful love.

TERIBAZUS.

Thou gen'rous Roman,
In gratitude I bow---she's here at hand;
A moment brings her to you, while at distance
I watch each avenue, each winding path,
That none intrude upon your privacy.---- [*Exit.*

RHADAMISTUS, *alone.*

At length I've seen my brother;---know how much
He differs from his father!—he shall seek
The Roman tents;—I'll there disclose myself;
There will embrace him with a brother's love.——
Oh! how the tender transport heaves and swells,
Till thus the fond excess disolves in tears!——

Enter MEGISTUS, *leading* ZENOBIA.

ZENOBIA.

Alas! my heart forebodes I know not what ——

MEGISTUS.

Dispel each doubt—this is your only refuge.——

ZENOBIA.

Thou gen'rous Roman,—if distress like mine——
If an unhappy captive may approach thee——

RHADAMISTUS.

To me affliction's voice—ye pow'rs of heav'n!
That air!—those features! that remember'd glance!

ZENOBIA.

If thus a wretch's presence can alarm you ——

RHADAMISTUS.

The music of that voice?—such once she look'd!

And if I had not plung'd her in the stream,——
I could persuade myself——

ZENOBIA.

Those well known accents!
Those tender soft regards!—nay mock me not!——
I could not hope to see thee—tell me—ar't thou——
That once ador'd!—oh!   *(faints into* Megistus' *arms.)*

MEGISTUS.

Ah! her strength forsakes her——
Support her heav'n!——   *(catches her in his arms.)*

RHADAMISTUS.

Ye wonder-working gods!
Is this illusion all? or does your goodness
Indeed restore her?—if I do not dream,
If this be true,—oh! let those angel-eyes
Open to life, to love, and Rhadamistus.

MEGISTUS.

What further miracles doth heav'n prepare?——

ZENOBIA.

Forgive my weakness---the air-painted image
Of my lov'd lord---and see!---again it's present!——
That look that speaks the fond impassion'd soul!
Yes, such he was!---oh! ar't thou---tell me---say——
Ar't thou restor'd me?---ar't thou Rhadamistus?——

RHADAMISTUS.

I have not murder'd her!---benignant gods!
I am not guilty---my Zenobia lives!——

ZENOBIA.

It is my lord---oh! I can hold no longer,——
But thus delighted spring to his embrace,
Thus wander o'er him with my tears and kisses,
And thus, and thus,---speak my enraptur'd soul.

RHADAMISTUS.

She lives! she lives! what kind protecting god,

Long

Long loft, and long lamented, gives thee back,
Gives me to view thee, and to hear thy voice
With joy to ecftacy, with tears to rapture?

ZENOBIA.

This good old man—'twas he preferv'd me for you,—

MEGISTUS.

Oh! day of charms!—oh! unexpected hour!
I have not liv'd in vain—thefe gufhing eyes
Have feen their mutual tranfports!——

RHADAMISTUS.

Gen'rous friend,
Come to my heart,—Zenobia's fecond father!—

ZENOBIA.

Thou art indebted more than thou can'ft pay him,—
Indebted for our infant babe preferv'd,
The bloffom of our joys!—thou can'ft not think
How much he looks, and moves, and talks like thee.——

RHADAMISTUS.

Oh! mighty gods!—it is too much of blifs,
Too exquifite to bear!—thefe barb'rous hands
Had well nigh murder'd both my wife and child!——
—Wilt thou forgive me—oh! my beft delight,
Wilt thou receive a traitor to your arms?
—Wilt thou Zenobia?

ZENOBIA.

Will I, gracious heav'n?
Thou fource of all my comfort!——

MEGISTUS.

Ha! beware,
Beware my prince!—but now with hafty ftep
I faw Tigranes circling yonder tent.

RHADAMISTUS.

Th' ambaffador of Rome he feeks, on bus'nefs
Of import high—I will prevent his fpeed——
—And muft I then fo foon depart Zenobia?

ZENOBIA,

ZENOBIA.

Hence, quickly hence—anon we'll meet again——

RHADAMISTUS.

Yes, we will meet; the gods have giv'n thee to me,
And they will finish their own holy work.   [*Exit.*

MEGISTUS.

My pray'rs are heard at length—Zenobia still
Shall be Armenia's queen.——

ZENOBIA.

Oh! good Megistus,
Heav'n has been bounteous, and restor'd my lord.—
With him I'll fly, wrapt in the gloom of night,
And thou, Megistus, thou shal't join our flight;
Plac'd near his throne thy gen'rous zeal shall share
The bright reward of all thy toil and care;
While I, redeem'd at length from fierce alarms,
Forget my woes in Rhadamistus' arms.

END OF THE THIRD ACT.

ACT the FOURTH.

Enter RHADAMISTUS, *and* TERIBAZUS.

TERIBAZUS.

THOU ar't a friend indeed, thou gen'rous man!
  The beſt of friends, to ſave ſuch innocence,
That lovely virgin bloom!---the pious act
Shall to remoteſt time tranſmit thy name,
Ennobled by humanity and virtue.

RHADAMISTUS.

Alas! no praiſe I merit;---'tis a deed
That loſes virtue's name------

TERIBAZUS.

Flamminius, no!
Thou ſhalt not derogate from worth like thine.
But oh! beware, my friend, and ſteel thy heart
Againſt the ſweet illapſe of gentler paſſions.
---To love her were ſuch treachery!---by heav'n!
It were a fraud of a more damned hue---
A fraud to ſacred friendſhip!---but my ſoul
Rejects the mean ſuſpicion---thou ar't juſt,
And Ariana ſhall be mine again!------

RHADAMISTUS.

If when the tumult of the war is paſs'd,
You then perſiſt to claim her------

TERIBAZUS.

Then perſiſt!
---When I do not perſiſt,---whene'er my heart
Forgets the fond idea---ha!---take heed---
Your colour dies by fits,---and now again
It fluſhes o'er your cheek---if beauty's pow'r
Can waken ſoft deſire,---and ſure ſuch beauty
May warm the breaſt of ſtoic apathy,------
If thou can'ſt love,---reſign the truſt at once.
For oh! to loſe her, to behold thoſe charms,

That

That all-perfection yielded to another,
Were the worst agony, the keenest stab
That ever pierc'd a lover to the soul.——
The thought,—the very thought inflames to madness!—

RHADAMISTUS.

(*Aside*) Not till the fever of his mind subsides,
Must I reveal me——the disclosure now
Would to his phrenzy give a whirlwind's wing,
And bury all in ruin——let her then,
Yes, Teribazus, let the blooming maid
Still in this camp, a voluntary captive,
——Since you will have it so——since weak mistrust
Can taint a noble spirit,——let her here
Teach that rare beauty to display its charms,
Its various graces;——bid those radiant eyes
Dart their quick glances to the tyrant's soul,
Inflame his hot desires, and half absolve them.

TERIBAZUS.

Madness and horror!——no!——haste, fly, begone,
And give her hence safe conduct——I can trust
To Roman continence——your Scipio's praise
Shall be the theme of fame's eternal lip!——

RHADAMISTUS.

Thou too attend her steps;——watch all her ways;
When we have reach'd the Roman sanctuary,
Then shall such wonders to thy list'ning ear,——
The web which fate has wove——beware my friend——
Tigranes comes——what would'st thou Sir?

Enter TIGRANES.

TIGRANES.

The king
Grants you one parley more——ev'n now this way
He bends his steps——remote from all he means
To hold a private conf'rence——

RHADAMISTUS.

Rome's ambassador
Attends his pleasure.—— [*Exit* Tigranes.

TERIBAZUS.

A TRAGEDY.

TERIBAZUS.

I must hence, Flamminius ———
Farewel!—yet e're thou go'st,—I still must crave
Another interview——farewel!——remember,
My love, my life, my all depend on thee.—— [*Exit.*

RHADAMISTUS.

Ah! luckless prince!—how lost in error's maze
Blindly he wanders, and love's sweet delusion
Infuses it's enchantment through his heart!
But when remov'd from Pharasmanes' pow'r
He learns my prior claim,—his gen'rous friendship
Will bound with transport at a brother's joys,
And with a warmth of sympathy partake 'em.
But ha!—my father!—grant me strength, ye pow'rs!
To meet the dread encounter. ———

Enter PHARASMANES.

PHARASMANES.

Once again
E're you depart, if Pharasmanes deign
To treat, and thus expostulate with Rome,
'Tis to thy pray'rs I grant it.

RHADAMISTUS.

Rome had father
Persuade than conquer—her well-ballanc'd justice——

PHARASMANES.

No more of Roman justice—blazon not
Virtues you ne'er have practis'd—with the name,
The specious name of love for human kind
You sanctify th' insatiate rage of conquest,
And where the sword has made a solitude,
That you proclaim a peace.—Ev'n now your views
Stand manifest to sight—To thee 'tis known
That Rhadamistus lives!———

RHADAMISTUS.

How Sir!—can he———
Does that unhappy prince ————

H   PHARASMANES.

PHARASMANES.

Thou falfe diffembler! ----
Yes in thy heart the fatal fecret's lodg'd !---

RHADAMISTUS.

Sir if your fon --- if you will fearch his heart ---

PHARASMANES.

From certain fugitives I've learn'd it all ---
In yonder camp, conceal'd from vulgar eyes,
To war againft his father ftill he lives !---
Why doft thou droop dejected?--- fomething lurks
Beneath that burning blufh---

RHADAMISTUS.

That burning blufh
Glows on my cheek for thee --- I know your fon,
And know him unfufceptible of guilt.

PHARASMANES.

Then, Roman, mark my words--- would'ft thou prevent
The carnage fate prepares on yonder plains?---
Go tell Paulinus I will treat of terms
With him, who brings me Rhadamiftus' head.

RHADAMISTUS.

Your own fon's head ! ---

PHARASMANES.

Why doft thou gaze fo earneft ?
Why thofe emotions ftruggling for a vent ?

RHADAMISTUS.

Amazement checks my voice, and loft in wonder
I view the unnatural father, who would bathe
His hands in blood,--- in a fon's blood--- a fon
Who pants, --- with ardor pants, --- on terms of peace
To fheathe the fword, and with a filial hand
To throw a veil over a father's crimes.

PHARASMANE

A TRAGEDY.

PHARASMANES.

By heav'n 'tis falfe — has he not dar'd to league
With my determin'd foes? —— ev'n to the fenate,
To ev'ry region, where his voice could pierce,
Has he not fled with the delufive ftory?
With grief and loud complaints inflam'd the world?
And even now, does not the ftripling come
To the Araxes' banks with Rome in arms?

RHADAMISTUS.

Tho' urg'd by dire conftraint, yet heav'n can witnefs
His ftrong reluctance.——

PHARASMANES.

Let the rebel know
He never fhall afcend Armenia's throne.

RHADAMISTUS.

And fhall deftruction with her horrid train
Stalk o'er the land?——

PHARASMANES.

Yes —— let deftruction loofe ——
'Tis Pharafmanes' glory ———

RHADAMISTUS.

Can the rage,
And the wild tumult of deftructive havoc
Adminifter delight? ——alas! ——the day
That deluges the land with human blood,
Is that a day of glory? ——— ——— ———
I, Sir, have travers'd o'er the field of death,
Where war had fpent its rage —— hadft thou beheld
That fcene of horror, —— where unnumber'd wretches,
In mangled heaps lay welt'ring in their gore;
Where the fond father in the gafp of death
Wept for his children, —— where the lover figh'd
For her, whom never more his eyes could view;
Where various mifery fent forth its groans;——
Had'ft thou beheld that fcene, — the touch of nature
Had ftirr'd within thee, and the virtuous drop
Of pity gufh'd unbidden from thy eye. —

PHARASMANES.

PHARASMANES.

Enervate slave!--- here ends all further parley---
Go tell your gen'ral, tell your Roman chiefs,
The father claims his son. --- Have we not heard
How your own Brutus to the lictor's sword
Condemn'd his children?--- and would Rome dispute
A king's paternal pow'r?--- let 'em yield up
The treach'rous boy, or terrible in arms
Shall Pharasmanes overwhelm their legions,
Mow down their cohorts, and their mangled limbs
Give to the vulture's beak.

RHADAMISTUS.

And yet reflect---

PHARASMANES.

Roman no more.-----

RHADAMISTUS.

Unwilling I withdraw;---
A father's stern resolve the son shall mourn,
And with a pang of nature shall behold
The Roman eagle dart like thunder on thee.   [*Exit.*

PHARASMANES, *alone.*

Away, and leave me slave!--- to-morrow's sun
Shall see my great revenge--- mean time I give
The gentle hours to love and Ariana.---
What ho! Tigranes!

Enter TIGRANES.

PHARASMANES.

Does the stubborn fair
Yield to my ardent vows?

TIGRANES.

She mocks your passion,
And gives to Teribazus all her smiles.

PHARASMANES.

By heav'n! ev'n love itself shall be my slave!---

---Yet

--- Yet love like mine requires her soft consent,
And will not riot o'er her plunder'd charms. ———
—Quick, bring her father to me———

TIGRANES.

By your orders
At hand Megistus waits your sov'reign will.   [*Exit.*

PHARASMANES.

Bring him before us — wise and prudent age
Will plead my cause, and second my desires.

Enter MEGISTUS.

MEGISTUS.

Dread Sir — a blameless, — a distress'd old man,
Of guilt unconscious ——-

PHARASMANES.

Whatsoe'er thy guilt
A smile from Ariana expiates all.

MEGISTUS.

Believe me, Sir, I never have offended ——
She was my sole delight; my age's comfort; ——
For her I felt more than a parent's love ——
But 'midst the troubles that distract the land
I lost her — in despair — with yearning heart
I rang'd the country round in fond pursuit ——
This is my crime --- sure 'tis no crime to love
Such blooming innocence! ——

PHARASMANES.

Dispel thy fears ——
Thy love for Ariana speaks thy virtue ——
That graceful form, that symmetry of shape,
That bloom, those features, those love-darting eyes,
All, all attract, that there each fond admirer
Could ever gaze, enamour'd of her charms.

MEGISTUS.

Alas! whate'er the symmetry of shape,

                                       Whate'er

Whate'er the grace that revels in her feature,
Glows in her bloom, or sparkles in her eye,
They all are transient beauties, soon to fade,
And leave inanimate that decent form.
Inward affliction saps the vital frame,
Incurable affliction!—fix'd in woe
Her eyes for ever motionless and dim
Gaze on the fancied image of her husband.

PHARASMANES.

Her husband!

MEGISTUS.

Yes; a husband sever'd from her
By fatal chance!—him she for ever sees
With fancy's gushing eye, and seeks him still
In fond excursions of delusive thought.
She pines each hour, and ev'n in blooming dies,
As drooping roses,—while the worm unseen
Preys on their fragrant sweets, still beauteous look,
And waste their aromatic lives in air.

PHARASMANES.

The rose transplanted to a warmer sky
Shall raise its languid head, and all be well.

MEGISTUS.

Her husband still survives, and far remote
He wanders in Armenia's realm——

PHARASMANES.

No more
To call her his!—by all my promis'd joys
His doom is fix'd!—do thou streight seek thy daughter,
My loveliest Ariana—in her ear
Breathe the mild accents of a father's voice,
And reconcile her heart to love and me.

MEGISTUS.

Your pardon, Sir,—it were not fit my voice
Should teach her to betray her holy vows.

PHARASMANES.

A TRAGEDY.

PHARASMANES.

When Pharasmanes speaks ———

MEGISTUS.

My life is his, ———
And when he wills it, 'tis devoted to him ———
But, Sir, tho' poor, — my honour still is mine,
'Tis all that heav'n has giv'n me, — and that gift
The gods expect I never should resign.

PHARASMANES.

And do'st thou hesitate?— what, when a crown
Invites thy daughter to imperial splendor?

MEGISTUS.

Oh! not for me such splendor!— I have liv'd
My humble days in virtuous poverty.
To tend my flock, to watch each rising flow'r,
Each herb, each plant that drinks the morning dew,
And lift my praise to the just gods on high!———
These were my habits, these my only cares;———
—These hands suffic'd to answer my desires,
And having naught, — yet naught was wanting to me.

PHARASMANES.

Away, thou slave! — I would not quite despise thee—
Or yield your daughter, or my swiftest vengeance
Falls on thy hoary head — a monarch's love
Shall seize her trembling to his eager arms,
Then spurn her back a prey to wan despair,
Till bitter anguish blast each wither'd charm,
And rave in vain for love and empire scorn'd!———
[*Exit.*

MEGISTUS, *alone.*

Fell monster go!— inexorable tyrant!———
Perhaps I should have sooth'd his lion rage
With feign'd compliance — ha! — why sudden thus———

Enter ZENOBIA.

ZENOBIA.

Th' important hour, Megistus, now approaches———
Lo!

Lo! the last blushes of departing day
But feebly streak yon dim horizon's verge.
My Rhadamistus comes to guide my steps ——
Thro' devious paths seek thou Zopiron's tent —
Thus we shall lull suspicion ——

MEGISTUS.

I obey; ——
May guardian angels spread their wings around thee! ——
[Exit:

ZENOBIA, *alone.*

Yes, the bless'd gods, who thro' the maze of fate
Have led us once again to meet in life,
Will prove the friends of virtue to the last.
— Ha! — Teribazus comes! ——

ZENOBIA, TERIBAZUS.

TERIBAZUS.

And is it giv'n
Once more to see thee here? — do'st thou avoid me?
Do'st thou despise me in this tender moment
When my soul bleeds with anguish at the thought
Of parting with thee? — Ariana! ——

ZENOBIA.

Oh! ——
Unhappy prince! — oh! fly me; shun me; death
And ruin follow — one short moment's stay
Will rouze your father's rage ——

TERIBAZUS.

My father's rage
Already has undone me — ah! in tears! ——
— And do they fall for me? — does that soft sigh
Heave for the lost, afflicted Teribazus? ——

ZENOBIA.

Yes the tear falls, and the sigh heaves for thee ——
Thy elegance of mind — the various graces
That bloom around thee, and adorn the hero, —
Nay, other ties there are which strongly plead,

And

And bid me tremble for thee.——
And yet,—sad recompense for all thy friendship,
To warn thee hence,—to bid thee shun my ways,
Is all the gratitude I now can offer.——

TERIBAZUS.

Thus must we part?——

ZENOBIA.

A rival is at hand,——
Here in the camp,—an unexpected rival,——
Sent by the gods,—the idol of my soul!

TERIBAZUS.

What say'st thou, Ariana?—has another
Usurp'd thy heart?—unkind, relentless maid!——
Since first thy beauty dawn'd upon my sight,
How have I lov'd,—repented,—yet lov'd on!——
Ev'n against you,—against myself I struggled——
Present I fled you—absent I ador'd——
I fled for refuge to the forest's gloom,——
But in the forest's gloom thy image met me!——
The shades of night, the lustre of the day,
All, all retrac'd my Ariana's form.——
Thy form pursued me in the battle's rage,
'Midst shouts, and all the clangor of the war.
—It stole me from myself!—my lonely tent
Re-ecchoes with my groans, and in the ranks
The wond'ring soldier hears my voice no more.

ZENOBIA.

Yet leave me Teribazus—gen'rous youth!
Remembrance oft shall dwell upon thy praise,
But for my love 'tis all another's claim.

TERIBAZUS.

Another's claim!—why wilt thou torture thus
A fond despairing wretch?—oh! not for me
Those sorrows fall—they are another's tears;——
—Another claims them from me—name this rival
That my swift fury—tell me has Flamminius,
Has the base Roman broke his promis'd faith?
Will not the barb'rous man afford you shelter?

ZENOBIA.

ZENOBIA,

ZENOBIA.

Why wilt thou force me speak?---the fate of all,
Thine Teribazus,---mine,---the fate of one,
Whom, were he known,---thy heart holds ever dear,
Is now concern'd---Flamminius claims my love------
Long since he won my heart------

TERIBAZUS.

Vindictive gods!
Flamminius claims thy love!------not Cæsar's self
Shall dare to wrest thee from me---Ariana!------
Thus on my knees,---would I could perish here---
That ev'n in death I still might gaze upon thee,
Till the last pang divide thee from my heart.

Enter RHADAMISTUS.

RHADAMISTUS.

It was the voice of anguish and despair!
Why thus illustrious prince------

TERIBAZUS.

(*Starting up*) Thou treach'rous Roman!---
Who com'st to violate each sacred tie,
The laws of honour, and the laws of love!
Who com'st beneath the mask of public faith
To do a robber's work!---

RHADAMISTUS.

When to your camp
I bring a heart that longs to serve you, prince,
Why this intemp'rate rage?---

TERIBAZUS.

To do the work
Of perfidy and fraud!---but first by rapine,
By violated maids your city grew;---
And do you come to emulate your sires?
Unwilling to degenerate in vice.---

RHADAMISTUS.

Mistaken youth!---oh! if you did but know me!
If you but knew the justice Rome intends---

TERIBAZUS.

TERIBAZUS.

Juſtice and Rome!—and doſt thou dare to join
Two names ſo oppoſite?—have we not heard
Of frugal conſuls, and of ſtoic chiefs,
Who ſoon forgetting here their ſabine farms,
Made war a trade, and then return'd to Rome
Rich with the plunder of the rifled eaſt?
Again ſome new Lucullus leads them on,
Fir'd with the love of rapine.—

RHADAMISTUS.

Fir'd with zeal
To break a nation's chains—would'ſt thou but hear me—
---It is a friend implores----

ZENOBIA.

A gen'rous friend!----
Then liſten to him---let theſe ſtreaming eyes,
Theſe earneſt pray'rs---this ſupplicating form----

TERIBAZUS.

Leagu'd with my foe behold her!---mighty gods!----
Have I deſerv'd it of her?----

RHADAMISTUS.

Yet be calm———
Yet liſten to me———Oh! I could unfold———
Yet ſtay—I'll prove myſelf a brother to thee.

TERIBAZUS.

Roman expect me in the battle's front----
Inſtant depart,----but leave thy prey behind;----
Dare not,---I charge thee dare not, tempt her hence----
To-morrow's ſun ſhall ſee me cloath'd in terror
Purſue thy ſteps thro' all the ranks of war,
Till my ſpear fix thee quiv'ring to the ground.   [*Exit.*

RHADAMISTUS, ZENOBIA.

ZENOBIA.

Yet, Rhadamiſtus, call him---let him know----

RHADAMISTUS.

RHADAMISTUS.

Thou lovely trembler!---banifh ev'ry fear----
The time now b ds us hence---and lo! the moon
Streams her mild radiance on the ruftling grove.----
---I will conduct thee---ha! Zopiron----

Enter ZOPIRON.

RHADAMISTUS.

Come
Thou beft of men, let me once more embrace thee.----

ZOPIRON.

Oh! fpeed thee hence---each moment's big with death---

RHADAMISTUS.

Farewel! farewel! when I've efcap'd your camp
Seek thou my brother; foothe his troubled fpirit,
Explain thefe wonders;---tell him Rhadamiftus
Efteems and loves, and honours all his virtues.----
Farewel Zopiron!---in Armenia's court
Thy king fhall thank thy goodnefs---my Zenobia,
Oh! let me guide thee from this place of danger
To life, to love, to liberty and joy.
[*Exit with* Zenobia.

ZOPIRON.

Lo! the heav'ns fmile with gentleft afpect on them!---
This calm ferene that ev'ry planet fheds
To light their fteps,---this glad ætherial mildnefs
Is fure the token of incircling gods
That hover anxious o'er the folemn fcene!----

Enter PHARASMANES, TIGRANES *following*.

PHARASMANES.

Let Teribazus ftreight attend our prefence---

TIGRANES.

But now with glaring eye and fierce demeanour
He enter'd yonder tent-----
PHARASMANES.

PHARASMANES.

Bid him approach us. ——
Then do thou round the midnight watch, and see
That Rome's ambassador has left my camp. [*Exit* Tigranes.
This war, Zopiron, shall be soon extinguish'd
In Roman blood, and yield Armenia to me.

ZOPIRON.

Armenia, Sir, still obstinately mourns
Lost Mithridates, father of his people.
Her hardy sons with one consenting voice
Demand a king from Rome;—all leagu'd and sworn
Never to crouch beneath the conqu'ror's yoke.

PHARASMANES.

But when the Roman eagle bites the ground,
They'll shrink aghast, and own my sov'reign sway.

Enter TERIBAZUS.

PHARASMANES.

Thou base confed'rate with thy father's foes!

TERIBAZUS.

The accusation, Sir,—if proof support it,
Gives you my forfeit life, and I resign it,
Freely resign—if destitute of proof,
It is a stab to honour,—and the charge
Should not be lightly urg'd.——

PHARASMANES.

This arrogance
That dictates to a father——

TERIBAZUS.

'Tis the spirit
Of injur'd innocence—if Pharasmanes
Suspect my truth,—send me where danger calls;—
Bid me this moment carry death and slaughter
To rage in yonder camp;——yes, then your son
Shall mark his hatred of the Roman name.

PHARASMANES.

PHARASMANES.

Haft thou not dar'd to thwart my tend'reſt paſſion,
And to ſeduce my Ariana's love?

TERIBAZUS.

And if this youthful heart, too prone to melt
At beauty's ray, receiv'd the gentle flame,
'Tis paſt—the charm is o'er—no longer now
I walk a captive in her haughty triumph!——
In vain ſhe now may call forth all her graces,
Inſtruct her eyes to roll with bidden fires,
And practice all the wonders of her face.
Ambition calls, and lights a nobler flame.

Enter TIGRANES.

TIGRANES.

Th' ambaſſador of Rome, and that old traitor
The falſe Megiſtus——

PHARASMANES.

Speak; unfold thy purpoſe.——

TIGRANES.

Together left the camp, and in their train
Bear Ariana with them——

TERIBAZUS.

Ariana!——
Have the ſlaves dar'd—deteſted treachery!
Now, now, my father, now approve my zeal.

PHARASMANES.

Haſte, fly, purſue her; bring the trait'reſs back!——

TERIBAZUS.

My rapid vengeance ſhall o'ertake their flight;
And bring the Roman plund'rer bound in chains. [*Exit.*

PHARASMANES.

Do thou, Tigranes, with a choſen band

A TRAGEDY.

Circle yon hills, and intercept their march.
And thou, Zopiron, send my swiftest horse
To range the wood, and sweep along the vale.
                                       [*Exit* Tigranes.

ZOPIRON.

Ye guardian deities, now lend your aid.   [*Exit.*

PHARASMANES, *alone.*

Has the perfidious,—yet ador'd deceiver,
Thus has she left me?—from a monarch's smile
Fled with a lawless ravager from Rome?——
Oh! give me vengeance; give Flamminius to me,
That he may die in agony unheard of.——
   The trait'ress then,—spite of each winning art,——
Spite of her guilt—she triumphs in my heart.

END OF THE FOURTH ACT.

ACT

ACT the FIFTH.

PHARASMANES.

NOT yet return'd!—I'm tortur'd on the rack——
By heav'n to-morrow's dawn——distracting thought!
E're that the Roman ravager enjoys
Her heav'n of bliss, and riots in delight.
My soul's on fire---this night I'll storm his camp
And dash his promis'd joys;---let loose my rage,
[*A flourish of trumpets.*
And bury all in ruin---ha!---what means
This new alarm?——

Enter TERIBAZUS, Soldiers, &c.

TERIBAZUS.

The treach'rous slave is taken!——
My speed outstripp'd him, and this arm that seiz'd
Hath well secur'd the traitor——

PHARASMANES.

Great revenge,
The measure of thy joys is full!——

TERIBAZUS.

At first
They made a feeble stand;---but hemm'd around
And close incircled by the sons of Asia
They saw death threat'ning at each javelin's point.
I rush'd upon Flamminius---much he courted
A secret parley, but my soul disdain'd
All further conf'rence---he and his complotter
The base Megistus, with the fair deserter
Remeasure back their steps, and clank their chains
In bitterness of heart. ----

PHARASMANES.

A father's thanks,
Shall well requite thee----lo! the traitors come----

Enter

Enter RHADAMISTUS, ZENOBIA, MEGISTUS, *in Chains.*

PHARASMANES.

Thou base perfidious!--- thou Italian plunderer!

RHADAMISTUS.

I do not mean to wage a war of words.---
Repent thee of this insult, of these chains
On him, who represents a people here.

PHARASMANES.

Anon thou'lt see how I respect that people.
My just revenge shall tell thee;--- on thy head,
And thine, Megistus, sudden vengeance falls.

MEGISTUS.

Alas! worn out with age and misery
I long to lay me in the shroud of death.

PHARASMANES.

I grant thy wish --- what words, fair fugitive,
Can colour thy deceit?----

ZENOBIA.

The heart resolv'd
Wants no excuse, no colouring of words ---
I found my husband,---flew to his embrace;---
This, --- this is he! --- the lord of my desires ---
With him content I'll traverse o'er the world.---

PHARASMANES.

Do'st thou avow it too?---

ZENOBIA.

Do I avow it?---
Yes, I exult, I glory in it--- Think'st thou
I'll prove so meanly false to honour's cause
As to apologize for being faithful?—

TERIBAZUS.

I see Flamminius has already school'd her
In Roman maxims ---

K   RHADAMISTUS.

RHADAMISTUS.

Miserable prince!
I will not answer thee--- too soon thy heart
For this last feat will bitterly reproach thee!---

TERIBAZUS.

Away with thy delusive arts --- if ever
I form alliance with haughty people,
Those ravagers of earth, --- if e'er again
I hold communion with thee, --- may the gods ---
May Pharasmanes, --- but it cannot be ---
My heart high beating in my country's cause,
Vows an eternal enmity with Rome.   [*Exit.*

RHADAMISTUS.

Thee, Pharasmanes, thee my voice addresses ---
Thou know'st my title to her --- Hymen's rites
Long since united both ——— Then loose these chains;—
'Tis in the name of Rome I ask it———

PHARASMANES.

Slave!———
Thy title, by the rights of war, is now extinguish'd.———
Captivity dissolves her former ties,
And now the laws of arms have made her mine.

ZENOBIA.

And are there laws to change the human heart?
To alter the affections of the soul?
Know that my heart is rul'd by other laws,
The laws of truth, of honour, and of love.
This is my husband! source of all my comfort!
With him I'll live— with him will dare to die!———

PHARASMANES.

By heav'n some mystery ——— thou treach'rous fair!
Mark well my words ——— unfold thy birth and rank—
My mind uncertain wanders in conjecture———
Who and what ar't thou?———Vain is ev'ry guess—
Resolve my doubts, or else the Roman's doom
Shall be determin'd streight———

ZENOBIA,

A TRAGEDY.

ZENOBIA.

And my resolve,
Tyrant, is fix'd to share my husband's fate.
That I unfold — that sentiment reveal —
To heav'n and earth reveal it —— for the rest
Guess if you can, — determine if you dare.

PHARASMANES.

Quick, drag Flamminius hence ———

RHADAMISTUS.

Slaves, hold your hands ———
My character protects me here ———

PHARASMANES.

Dispatch,
Instant dispatch, and seize Megistus too ——
[*Megistus is led off.*

ZENOBIA.

Horror! — call back the word — it shall not be —
Here will I hold him — barb'rous ruffians hold —
Murder! — my life! my lord! my husband! oh! —
[*Rhadamistus is dragg'd off.*

PHARASMANES.

Give him the torture; let your keenest pangs
Extort each secret from him ————

ZENOBIA.

Pharasmanes!
Thus lowly humbled, prostrate in the dust,
Washing your feet with tears — have mercy! — this
Will be the blackest, worst of all your murders —

PHARASMANES.

There's but one way to mitigate his doom —

ZENOBIA.

Give me to know it — spare him — spare his life —

PHARASMANES.

Abjure the slave, and by connubial vows
This instant make thee partner of my throne.

ZENOBIA.

My faith, my love, my very life is his—
My child is his—oh! think thou see'st my infant
Lifting his little hands—

PHARASMANES.

I'll hear no more—
Or yield this moment, or the traitor dies.

[*Exit* Pharasmanes.

ZENOBIA, *alone.*

Inhuman Tyrant!—madness seize my brain—
Swallow me earth——here shall these desp'rate hands
Strike on thy flinty bosom,—here my voice
Pierce to thy center,—till with pity touch'd
Your caverns open wide to hide a wretch
From hated men,—from misery like this.—

Enter TERIBAZUS.

Afflicted mourner, raise thee from the earth.

ZENOBIA.

What voice is that---I know thee well---thou ar't
That fiend accurst, the murd'rous Teribazus!---
Yes thou art welcome! *(rising)* thou delight'st in blood---
I am your willing victim---plunge your sword
Deep in my heart--- I'll thank thee for the stroke,
Since thou hast murder'd all my soul held dear.

TERIBAZUS.

Assuage this storm of grief, nor blame a lover
That dotes like me——could I behold that form
Snatch'd from my arms?——

ZENOBIA.

You know not what you've done——
Your blameless brother——

TERIBAZUS.

TERIBAZUS.

How!

ZENOBIA.

You've murder'd him ——
Your brother Rhadamiſtus ——

TERIBAZUS.

Rhadamiſtus! ——

ZENOBIA.

By thee he dies — that is your ſplendid deed ——

TERIBAZUS.

What ſay'ſt thou? — he my brother — urge me not
To inſtant madneſs — is he — tell me — ſay —
Ar't thou Zenobia? ——

ZENOBIA.

Yes, that fatal wretch! ——

TERIBAZUS.

If this be ſo —— what had I done, ye pow'rs!
To merit this extremity of woe ——
— Why did'ſt thou hide the awful ſecret from me? ——

ZENOBIA.

Could I betray him — could I truſt your father,
Whoſe fell ambition, whoſe relentleſs rage,
Has fix'd a price on our devoted heads?

TERIBAZUS.

Then ſhall this hated being — no! — I'll live
To ſave a brother ſtill — he ſhall not die —
Oh! let me ſeek him, --- throw me at his feet,
Implore forgiveneſs, and protract his days.

[*Exit* Teribazus.

ZENOBIA,

It is in vain --- he's loſt --- we both muſt periſh ——
And then my child --- who then ſhall guard his youth?

No more thefe eyes fhall fee him --- my fweet boy
Will break his heart, and unregarded die.——

Enter ZOPIRON.

ZOPIRON.

All's loft! all ruin'd! --- to the cave of death
Ev'n now the guards lead Rhadamiftus forth.

ZENOBIA.

Thou fee'ft the fad reverfe!—— immortal fpirits,——
Ye winged virtues, --- that with pitying eye
Watch the afflicted, --- will ye not infpire
In this fad hour,—— one great, one glorious thought,
Above the vulgar flight of common fouls,
To fave at once my hufband and my child?-----
--- The infpiration comes! --- the bright idea
Expands my heart, and charms my glowing foul.

ZOPIRON.

My gracious queen, let not a blind defpair ------

ZENOBIA.

Talk not, Zopiron, when the god infpires!
The god! the god! --- my heart receives him all ---
---- My lord, my Rhadamiftus ftill fhall live. [*Exit.*

ZOPIRON.

Yet, I conjure thee, hear thy faithful flave.——
[*Follows her out.*

Enter RHADAMISTUS, *and* Guards.

RHADAMISTUS.

Say, whither do you lead me? --- does your tyrant
Repent his horrid outrage?

Enter TERIBAZUS.

Guards withdraw
To a remoter ground ---- [*Exeunt Soldiers.*

A TRAGEDY.

RHADAMISTUS, TERIBAZUS.

RHADAMISTUS.

Mistaken prince!
My heart bleeds for thee ———

TERIBAZUS.

Oh! too well I know
The depth of guilt in which the fates have plung'd me.
--- I cannot look upon thee ----

RHADAMISTUS.

Oh! my brother,
Thus let me, ev'n in ruin, thus embrace thee.----

TERIBAZUS.

Do'st thou forgive me?--- could I e'er have thought
To see thee here? my rashness has undone thee!----

RHADAMISTUS.

No, thou art innocent --- the guilt is mine,
The guilt of mean, ungenerous policy
Of selfish wisdom, disingenuous art
That from a friend kept back the fatal secret,
When with the ardor of unbounded confidence,
I should have rush'd with transport to thy arms,
Unbosom'd all, and wrapt thee in my heart.

TERIBAZUS.

Alas! I've heap'd these horrors on your head ----
I've seal'd thy doom --- that is a brother's gift ----
The first essay of Teribazus' friendship! ---
But I am doom'd to be a wretch abhorr'd,
Of men and gods abhorr'd! --- doom'd like my father
To drench these murd'rous hands in brother's blood!----

RHADAMISTUS.

Imbitter not the pangs that rive my soul ---
Where is Zenobia?--- unrelenting pow'rs!
Was it for this your persecuting wrath
Gave me to meet her, gave that angel-sweetness
To these delighted eyes, these eager arms?

TERIBAZUS.

TERIBAZUS.

I'll give you freedom still --- by heav'n I will ---

RHADAMISTUS.

Was she but giv'n me to afflict her more?
To wake in that dear breast a gleam of joy,
A mockery of joy, --- joy scarce, ye pow'rs!
Divided by the moment of delight
From black despair, from agony and death?

TERIBAZUS.

I will protect her, --- will restore her to thee,
Or do a deed shall strike mankind with horror!
Not ev'n a father shall retard my sword ---
In his own blood I'll drench it ---

RHADAMISTUS.

Ha! ----

TERIBAZUS.

This hand,
E're thou shalt fall a victim to his fury,
Shall to the heart, --- th' inhuman heart of him ---
Who dares ----

RHADAMISTUS.

No more of that --- can I consent,
That a brave gen'rous youth, a much lov'd brother,
For ev'ry virtue fam'd, --- shall thus debase
By an atrocious deed his fair renown,
And perpetrate a dark insidious work?
--- Oh! I should well deserve the worst of ills ---
--- I then should justify a father's cruelty! ----

TERIBAZUS.

He has undone thee --- has undone us all ---
But yet thou shalt not die --- by heav'n I swear ---
Yes, take me, horror! pour into my heart
Thy blackest purpose --- nerve my lifted arm
To dash him headlong from his glitt'ring throne
A terrible example to the world.

RHADAMISTUS.

RHADAMISTUS.

Beware, beware, my brother --- yet reflect ---
You would strike vice with terror --- tell me then,
Would not the act of rash impetuous zeal,
Would not th' example arm the ruffian's hand?
Thy virtue thus inflames thy gen'rous ardor ---
But oh! my brother, let it not be said
That virtue ever held the murd'rer's knife!

TERIBAZUS.

Gods! have I ruin'd such unheard of goodness?
Swift I'll dispatch a message to Paulinus,
And call his legions to assault the camp——

Enter TIGRANES, *and* Guards.

TIGRANES.

Guards, seize your pris'ner --- in a dungeon's gloom
Plunge him sequester'd from the light of heav'n.
'Tis Pharasmanes' will——

TERIBAZUS.

Thou medling fiend!
I will attend his steps; will still protect him
From men like thee——

RHADAMISTUS.

Should Pharasmanes dare
To violate the rights of public law,
Rome is at hand, and will have ample vengeance.
[*Exit with* Teribazus.

TIGRANES.

My thirst of vengeance shall be sated first.——
Yes, guard him, prince; it makes thy ruin sure!
Thy Ariana too, while fate is busy,
Shall meet her doom, and leave my road to glory
All smooth and level to ambition's wish.

Enter ZOPIRON.

ZOPIRON.

'Gainst Rome's ambassador the king, Tigranes,

L   Suspends

Suspends his sentence till his further orders.
The qeen commands it too.

TIGRANES.

The queen!---what queen?

ZOPIRON.

The beauteous Ariana; now your sovereign.

TIGRANES.

Has she relented?---is she married to him?

ZOPIRON.

She is---the scene with various passions burn'd!---
Her tresses all unbound, with faded charms,
Yet lovely ev'n in sorrow, thro' the ranks
Eager she flew, with shrieks, with outstretch'd arms,
Invoking ev'ry god!---the wond'ring soldier
With soften'd sinews, dropt the sword to earth
And gaz'd with mix'd emotions as she pass'd.
Prone to the ground at Pharasmanes' feet
She fell---he rais'd her soon, and smil'd consent----
To the king's tent she press'd with eager speed----
Th' exulting monarch call'd his priests around him,
And soon with solemn march and festive song
In his pavillion sought the blooming bride.

TIGRANES.

This sudden change, Zopiron, this rash haste,
I like it not----

ZOPIRON.

Nor I Tigranes: doubt,
Suspicion, fear, and wonder, and mistrust,
Rise in each anxious thought———

TIGRANES.

But did'st thou see
The ceremony clos'd?———

ZOPIRON.

I did:—at first
All pale and trembling Ariana stood.

Then

A TRAGEDY.

Then more collected, with undaunted step
She to the altar bore the nuptial cup.
There reverent bow'd, and "hear ye gods," she said,
"Hear and record the purpose of my soul."
With trembling lips then kiss'd the sacred vase,
And as our country's solemn rites require,
Drank of the hallow'd liquor.—From her hand
The king receiv'd it, and with eager joy,
As to his soul he took the nectar'd draught,
With stedfast eye she view'd him, whilst a smile
Of sickly joy gleam'd faintly o'er her visage.

TIGRANES.

Well, she's our queen—the diadem is hers ———

ZOPIRON.

How long to wear it, heav'n alone can tell. ———

[*The back scene draws, and discovers the king's pavillion, with an altar, and fire blazing on it; soft musick is play'd, and they come forward.*

PHARASMANES *and* ZENOBIA.

PHARASMANES.

At length my Ariana's soft compliance
Endears the present bliss, and gives an earnest
Of joy to brighten a long train of years.

ZENOBIA.

Alas! fond man expatiates oft in fancy,
Unconscious of the fates, and oft in thought
Anticipates a bliss he ne'er enjoys.

PHARASMANES.

Away with gloomy care; for thou ar't mine,
Thou, Ariana!—all our future days
Shall smile with gay, with ever-young desire,
And not a cloud o'ercast the bright serene.

ZENOBIA.

And does thy penetrating eye pervade
What time has yet in store?

PHARASMANES.

PHARASMANES.

Why doſt thou aſk?

ZENOBIA.

I have been us'd to grief—releaſe the Roman,
And give him hence ſafe conduct to his friends;———
I then ſhall be at peace.————

PHARASMANES.

Beware, beware!
Nor rouze again the pangs, that fire a ſoul,
Which fiercely doats like mine.

ZENOBIA.

Diſmiſs him hence;
Give him his life—it was your marriage vow
He ſhould not ſuffer—let me ſee him firſt;———
Grant me one interview,—one little hour;
In that poor ſpace I can crowd all that's left me
Of love, and tenderneſs, and fond concern,
Before we part for ever————

PHARASMANES.

Fond concern!
And love, and tenderneſs!—and ſhall the Roman
Uſurp a monarch's due?——that look betrays
The ſecret workings of a heart eſtrang'd!
And ſhall the man, who dares diſpute my love,
Shall the ſlave breathe a moment?——haſte, Tigranes,
And ſee immediate execution on him.   [*Exit* Tigranes.

ZENOBIA.

Oh! ſtay Tigranes—barb'rous man, recall
The horrid mandate———

PHARASMANES.

By immortal love,
I ſee the ſlave ſtill triumphs in your heart.

ZENOBIA.

Oh! ſpare him, ſpare him———by the vital air,
By your own promis'd faith———   [*Kneels to him.*

PHARASMANES.

A TRAGEDY.

PHARASMANES.

Since lov'd by thee
His doom is doubly feal'd. ⸺

ZENOBIA.

You shall not fly me⸺
Now tear me, drag me groveling in the dust,
Tear off these hands — tear, tear me peice-meal first —

PHARASMANES.

Nay, then since force must do it ⸻   [*Shakes her off.*

ZENOBIA.

Barb'rous tyrant!   [*She lies stretch'd on the ground.*

PHARASMANES.

I go to see the minion of your heart
Expire in pangs before me⸺ ha! ⸺ what means
This more than winter's frost that chills my veins?⸺

ZENOBIA.

(*Looking up*) That groan revives, and calls me back to life!⸺

PHARASMANES.

I cannot move⸺ each vital function's lost ⸺
The purple current of my blood is stopt⸺
I freeze⸺ I burn⸺ oh! 'tis the stroke of death⸺
                                [*Falls on the ground.*

ZENOBIA.

(*Rising*) Yes, tyrant, yes; it is the stroke of death
And I inflict it⸺ I have done it all⸺

PHARASMANES.

Pernicious trait'ress! thou!⸺

ZENOBIA.

My vengeance did it ⸺
Zenobia's vengeance! ⸺ 'tis Zenobia strikes⸺
Zenobia executes her justice on thee!⸺

PHARASMANES.

PHARASMANES.

Oh! dire accurst event!---ar't thou Zenobia?

ZENOBIA.

Yes, thou fell monster, know me for Zenobia!
Know the ambassador is Rhadamistus!
Haste thee, Zopiron, and proclaim him king.
[*Exit* Zopiron.

PHARASMANES.

May curses light upon thee—oh! I die,
And racks and wheels disjoint me——

ZENOBIA.

Writhe in torment,
In fiercer pangs than my dear father knew.
—But I revenge his death—I dash'd the cup
With precious poison!—(*a flourish of trumpets*) ha!—now tyrant wake,
And hear those sounds—my Rhadamistus reigns!——

PHARASMANES.

What and no help!—it is too late—the fates,
The fiends surround me—more than Ætna's fires
Burn in my veins—yet heav'n—no—'tis in vain——
I cannot rise—my crimes—my tenfold crimes——
They pull me!—oh!—— [*Dies.*

ZENOBIA.

There fled the guilty spirit,
Shade of my father view your daughter now!
Behold her struggling in a righteous cause!
Behold her conqu'ring in the tyrant's camp!
Behold your murd'rer levell'd in the dust!——

A second flourish of trumpets.

RHADAMISTUS.

(*Within the scenes*) Where is Zenobia?——

ZENOBIA.

Rhadamistus, here!——

Enter

A TRAGEDY.

Enter RHADAMISTUS, TERIBAZUS, MEGISTUS, ZOPIRON, &c.

RHADAMISTUS.

Oh! let me, let me thus,—thus pour my foul,
Thus fpeak my joy,—thus melt within thy arms.——

ZENOBIA.

My lord! my life, my Rhadamiftus!—come,
Grow to my heart,--that bounds and fprings to meet thee.—

RHADAMISTUS.

Once more reviv'd and fnatch'd again from death
Thus do I fee thee?—thefe are fpeechlefs joys,
And tears alone exprefs them——

ZENOBIA.

Have I fav'd thee?
All-gracious gods! 'tis rapture in th' extreme!——

RHADAMISTUS.

My fweet deliverer! my all of blifs!——

ZENOBIA.

Oh! it is joy too exquifite!—and yet
Grief will imbitter ecftacy like this!——
There lies your father!

RHADAMISTUS.

All his crimes
Be buried with him!—nature will have way,
And o'er his corfe thus fheds the filial tear.

TERIBAZUS.

Oh! that my tears could wafh away his ftains!——

ZENOBIA.

Wilt thou forgive his murderer?——

RHADAMISTUS.

For thee,
Befet with wrongs, and injur'd as thou wer't,

In

In ev'ry region fame shall clap her wings,
And the recording muse applaud thy virtue.

ZENOBIA.

If thou forgiv'st me, I am bless'd indeed!
Now we shall part no more—Megistus too!—
Thou good old man!—let me embrace thee—ha!

MEGISTUS.

The blood forsakes her cheek—her eyes are fix'd!—

ZENOBIA.

Support me—help me—oh! I die—I die.——
[*Falls in* Megistus' *arms.*

RHADAMISTUS.

She faints—her colour dies—revive Zenobia;—
Revive my love;—thy Rhadamistus thus,
Thus calls your flutt'ring spirit back to life.

ZENOBIA.

It will not be—the toil of life is o'er—
My Rhadamistus—   [*Sinks down on the ground.*

RHADAMISTUS.

Must I lose thee then?—

ZENOBIA.

Oh! the envenom'd cup!—the marriage rites
Requir'd that I should drink it first myself—
There was no other way—I did it freely
To save thy life—to save thee for my child.—

RHADAMISTUS.

A'rt thou a victim for a wretch like me?
Is there no antidote to stop the course
Of this vile poison?—

ZENOBIA.

None—it rages now—
It rages thro' my veins---my eyes grow dim----
                                      They're

A TRAGEDY.

They're loſt in darkneſs—oh!—I cannot ſee thee—
Where art thou, Rhadamiſtus?—muſt I breathe
Longer in life,—and never ſee thee more!—
And are my eyes forbid one dear farewell?
Oh! cruel ſtars!—muſt they not fix on thee
The laſt expiring glance?——

RHADAMISTUS.

Relentleſs pow'rs!
There lies Zenobia!——round that pallid beauty
Call your ætherial hoſt, each winged virtue,
Call ev'ry angel down,—bid 'em behold
That matchleſs excellence, and then refuſe
Soft pity if they can!——

ZENOBIA.

Megiſtus,—ſeek my child,—
And bring him to his father—Rhadamiſtus,—
—Wilt thou protect him?——My ſweet orphan-babe
I leave thee too!——oh! train him up in virtue—
Wilt thou be fond of him——a mother's fondneſs
My child ſhould meet——oh! raiſe me, Rhadamiſtus—
Give me thy hand——my little infant——oh!——
[*Dies.*

RHADAMISTUS.

Tears, you do well to ſtop—your wretched drops
Are unavailing at a ſight like this!——
And art thou gone?——ah! 'thus defac'd and pale,
Thus do I ſee thee?——is that ghaſtly form
All that is left me of thee?——give me daggers,
—Give me ſome inſtant means of death, my friends,
That I may throw this load of life away,
And let our hearts be both inurn'd together.

TERIBAZUS.

Live, live my brother, for your infant ſon—
Let him prevail——

RHADAMISTUS.

Inhuman that thou art!
Think you I'll ſtay impriſon'd here in life,
When there—behold her——how ſhe ſmiles in death!—

When

When there that form —— think ye I'll linger here?---—
Dead, dead Zenobia!—ſtill I have thee thus——
You ne'er ſhall part us——this at leaſt I'll hold,
And cling for ever to theſe pale, pale charms;
Here breathe my laſt, and faithful ſtill in death,
Love ſhall unite us in one peaceful grave.

MEGISTUS.

Now, old Megiſtus, gods! has liv'd too long!---—

TERIBAZUS.

Bring ev'ry aid, all medicinal ſkill
To call a wretched brother back to life,
And give each lenient balm to woes like his.
From thee ambition, what misfortunes flow?
To thee what varied ills weak mortals owe?
'Twas this for years laid deſolate the land,
And arm'd againſt a ſon the father's hand;
To black deſpair poor loſt Zenobia drove;
The hapleſs victim of diſaſtrous love!---—

EPILOGUE:

Written by DAVID GARRICK, Esq;

And Spoken by Mrs. ABINGTON.

(She peeps thro' the Curtain)

HOW do you all, good folks?—In tears for certain,
I'll only take a PEEP BEHIND THE CURTAIN;
You're all so full of tragedy, and sadness!
For me to come among ye, would be madness:
This is no time for giggling—when you've leisure,
Call out for me, and I'll attend your pleasure;
As soldiers hurry at the beat of drum,
Beat but your hands, that instant I will come.
               [*She enters upon their clapping.*
This is so good, to call me out so soon——
The COMIC MUSE by me intreats a BOON;
She call'd for PRITCHARD, her first maid of honour,
And begg'd of her to take the task upon her;
But she,—I'm sure you'll all be sorry for't,
Resigns her place, and soon retires from court:
To bear this loss, we courtiers make a shift,
When good folks leave us, worse may have a lift.
   The COMIC MUSE, whose ev'ry smile is grace,
And her STAGE SISTER, with her tragic face,
Have had a quarrel——each has writ a CASE.
And on their friends assembled now I wait,
To give you of THEIR DIFFERENCE A TRUE STATE.
MELPOMENE, complains when she appears, ——
For five good acts, in all her pomp of tears,
To raise your souls, and with her raptures wing 'em,
Nay wet your handkerchiefs, that you may wring 'em.
Some flippant hussey, like myself comes in;
Crack goes her fan, and with a giggling grin,
Hey! PRESTO PASS!—all topsy turvy see,
For HO, HO, HO! is chang'd to HE, HE, HE!
We own the fault, but 'tis a fault in vogue,
'Tis theirs, who call and bawl for—EPILOGUE!
                                  O! shame

EPILOGUE.

O! shame upon you——for the time to come,
Know better---and go miserable home.
What says our COMIC GODDESS?——with reproaches,
She vows her SISTER TRAGEDY encroaches!
And spite of all her virtue, and ambition,
Is known to have an am'rous disposition:
For in FALSE DELICACY---wond'rous sly,
Join'd with a certain IRISHMAN---O fye!
She made you, when you ought to laugh, to cry.----
Her sister's smiles with tears she try'd to smother,
Rais'd such a tragi-comic kind of pother,
You laugh'd with one eye, while you cry'd with t'other.
What can be done?---sad work behind the scenes!
There comic females scold with tragic queens.
Each party different ways the foe assails,
These shake their daggers, those prepare their nails.
'Tis YOU alone must calm these dire mishaps,
Or we shall still continue pulling caps.
What is your will?---I read it in your faces;
That all hereafter take their proper places,
Shake hands, and kifs and friends, and--BURN THEIR CASES.

FINIS.

THE GRECIAN DAUGHTER

A

TRAGEDY:

As it is acted at the

THEATRE-ROYAL

IN

DRURY-LANE.

A NEW EDITION.

LONDON:
Printed for W. GRIFFIN, at GARRICK'S-HEAD,
in Catherine Street, Strand.
MDCCLXXII.

THE
GRECIAN DAUGHTER.
A TRAGEDY.
As it is acted at the
THEATRE-ROYAL
in
DRURY-LANE.

LONDON:
Printed for W. GRIFFIN, at GARRICK'S Head,
in Catherine Street, Strand.
MDCCLXXII.

TO
Mrs. BARRY,

(With the Printed Copy of the GRECIAN DAUGHTER)

From the AUTHOR.

ENchanting Genius! Siren of the age;
Oh! form'd to animate a drooping stage!
Bless'd in thy talents; Matchless in thy art!
Delightful Tyrant of the feeling heart!
This Play be thine; accept the Poet's praise,
And still endure the scenes you help'd to raise.
    Britain and France shall now the laurel share;
Thou CLAIRON here, and She a BARRY there!
Proceed, Great Actress! Friend of ev'ry Muse!
The NINE without Thee half their rapture lose.
Fair Virtue's image THEY can only trace;
THOU giv'st her form, and harmony, and grace.
In human shape (what PLATO wish'd to see),
She walks the stage, she breathes, she charms in Thee.
Proceed each night to draw the tender tear,
Please ev'ry eye, and ravish ev'ry ear.
Nor let the pride of a too selfish age
Damp with unhallow'd sounds thy native rage.
Ah! let not surly wealth thy art degrade,
And call its influence a MERE MIMIC TRADE.
THINE IS THE ART, which TULLY priz'd of yore,
Himself instructed by theatric lore;
THINE IS THE ART DEMOSTHENES admir'd,
Th' Athenian state when his BOLD ACTION fir'd;
Aloft, LIKE THINE, when his extended hand
Menac'd the proud oppressors of the land;
And, nerv'd by feelings equal to thy own,
Made HAUGHTY PHILIP tremble on his throne.

                                       Go,

Go, fair Enthusiast! with thy magic skill
Mould the obedient Passions to thy will.
The Passions, pliant to thy sov'reign sway,
Alternate rise, blend, mix, and melt away.
Shew how Euphrasia, of affections mild,
Doats on her Sire, her Husband, and her Child.
Sweet fall the accents—Oh! let stilness reign,
While the soft Warbler pours her plaintive strain!
Sweet fall the accents, meek as ev'ry grace
That decks that Form, and beams around the Face.
Then rising higher, urg'd by Nature's laws,
Brave ev'ry danger in a Father's cause.
With pilgrim feet ascend the craggy steep;
There might the night-bird listen as you weep.
Thence to the tyrant, wing thy rapid way,
And shake his soul with terror and dismay.
Alarm'd, distracted, wild with madd'ning fears,
" Amaze the faculties of eyes and ears."
To vengeance rouz'd, charming in horror shine,
And bid e'en BRUTUS' dagger envy thine.

Lovely assassin!—Hark! with loud acclaim
Consenting Theatres attest thy fame!
Delighted hear thee, with true genius fraught,
Give weight to words, and energy to thought.
Wak'd by thy voice, to life each Muse shall spring,
" What Muse for BARRY can refuse to sing?"
WHITEHEAD once more shall form the just design,
And tune the note, almost as sweet as thine;
MASON be tempted to unlock his store,
And his lov'd CHORUS meditate no more.
Then may we view, to claim the Poet's prize,
New SOUTHERNS, ROWES, and other OTWAYS rise;
A SHAKESPEARE comes but once from the indulgent skies.
These scenes no longer shall attract thy eye,
Poor lost EUPHRASIA thrown neglected by.
A FEMALE-GARRICK Britain's stage shall see,
And e'en the BARD owe half his fame to THEE.

PROLOGUE.

Spoken by Mr. WESTON.

He peeps in at the Stage Door.

HIP! mufic! mufic!—Have you more to play?
Somewhat I'd offer——Stop your cat-gut, pray.

Will you permit, and not pronounce me rude,
A bookfeller one moment to intrude?
My name is Foolfcap:—Since you faw me laft,
Fortune hath given me a rare helping caft.
To all my toils a wife hath put a ftop——
A devil then; but now I keep a fhop.
My mafter died, poor man!—He's out of print!
His widow,—fhe had eyes, and took my hint.
A prey to grief, fhe could not bear to be,
And fo turn'd over a new leaf with me.

I drive a trade; have authors in my pay,
Men of all work, per week, per fheet, per day.
TRAV'LLERS—who not one foreign country know:
And PAST'RAL POETS—in the found of Bow.
TRANSLATORS—from the Greek they never read;
CANTABS and SOPHS—in Covent-Garden bred.
HISTORIANS, who can't write;—who only take
Sciffars and pafte;—cut, vamp; a book they make.

I've treated for this play; can buy it too,
If I could learn what you intend to do.
If for nine nights you'll bear this tragic ftuff;
I have a newfpaper, and there can puff.

A newfpaper does wonders!—None can be
In debt, in love, dependent or quite free,
Ugly or handfome, well, or ill in bed,
Single or married, or alive or dead,
But we give life, death, virtue, vice with eafe;
In fhort a newfpaper does what we pleafe.

There jealous authors at each other bark;
Till Truth leaves not one glimpse, no, not one spark;
But lies meet lies, and jostle in the dark.
Our bard within has often felt the dart
Sent from our quiver, levell'd at his heart.
I've press'd him, ere he plays this desp'rate game,
To answer all, and vindicate his name.
But he convinc'd that all but truth must die,
Leaves to its own mortality the lie.
Would any know,—while parties fight pell-mell,
How he employs his pen?—his play will tell.
To That he trusts; That he submits to you,
Aim'd at your tend'rest feelings,—moral,—new.
The scenes, he hopes, will draw the heart-felt tear;
Scenes that come home to ev'ry bosom here.

  If this will do, I'll run and buy it straight;
Stay—Let me see;—I think I'd better wait——
Yes;—I'll lie snug, till you have fix'd it's fate.

EPILOGUE.

Written by a Friend.

And Spoken by Miss YOUNGE.

THE Grecian Daughter's compliments to all;
Begs that for Epilogue you will not call;
For leering, giggling would be out of season,
And hopes by me you'll hear a little reason.
  A father rais'd from death, a nation sav'd,
A tyrant's crimes by female spirit brav'd,
That tyrant stabb'd, and by her nerveless arm,
While Virtue's spell surrounding guards could charm!

Can

EPILOGUE.

Can she, this sacred tumult in her breast,
Turn Father, Freedom, Virtue, all to Jest?
Wake you, ye fair ones, from your sweet repose;
As wanton zephyrs wake the sleeping rose;
Dispel those clouds, which o'er your eyelids crept,
Which our wise Bard mistook, and swore you wept.
Shall she to MACARONIES life restore,
Who yawn'd, half dead, and curs'd the tragic BORE?
Dismiss 'em, smirking, to their nightly haunt,
Where dice and cards their moon-struck minds enchant?
Some muffled, like the witches in Macbeth,
Brood o'er the magic circle, pale as death!
Others, *the cauldron go about—about—*
And Ruin enters, as the Fates run out!
   Bubble, bubble,
   Toil and trouble,
   Passions burn,
  And bets are double!
   Double! double!
   Toil and trouble;
   Passions burn,
   And all is bubble!
But jests apart, for scandal forms these tales;
Falsehood be mute—let Justice hold her scales:
Britons were ne'er enslav'd by evil pow'rs;
To peace, and wedded love, they give their midnight hours;
From slumbers pure, no rattling dice can wake 'em!
Who *make* the laws, were never known to *break* 'em.
'Tis false, ye fair, whatever Spleen may say,
That you down Folly's tide are borne away;
You never wish at deep distress to sneer;
For eyes, tho' bright, are brighter thro' a tear.
 Should it e'er be this Nation's wretched fate
To laugh at all that's good, and wise, and great;
Arm'd at all points, let Genius take the field,
And on the stage afflicted Virtue shield,
Drive from the land each base unworthy passion,
Till Virtue triumph in despite of Fashion.

Dramatis Personæ.

EVANDER,	Mr. BARRY.
PHILOTAS,	Mr. REDDISH.
MELANTHON,	Mr. AICKIN.
PHOCION,	Mr. J. AICKIN.
DIONYSIUS,	Mr. PALMER.
ARCAS,	Mr. HURST.
GREEK HERALD,	Mr. PACKER.
CALIPPUS,	Mr. INCHBALD.
GREEK SOLDIER,	Mr. DAVIES.
OFFICER,	Mr. WHEELER.
EUPHRASIA,	Mrs. BARRY.
ERIXENE,	Miss PLATT.

Scene, SYRACUSE.

THE
GRECIAN DAUGHTER.

ACT I.

Enter MELANTHON, *and* PHILOTAS.

MELANTHON.

YET, yet a moment; hear, Philotas, hear me!
Phil. No more; it must not be.
Melan. Obdurate man;
Thus wilt thou spurn me, when a king distress'd,
A good, a virtuous, venerable king,
The father of his people, from a throne
Which long with ev'ry virtue he adorn'd,
Torn by a ruffian, by a tyrant's hand,
Groans in captivity? In his own palace
Lives a sequester'd prisoner?—Oh! Philotas,
If thou hast not renounc'd humanity;
Let me behold my sovereign; once again
Admit me to his presence, let me see
My royal master.
  Phil. Urge thy suit no further;
Thy words are fruitless; Dionysius' orders
Forbid access; he is our sov'reign now;
'Tis his to give the law, mine to obey.
  Melan. Thou can'st not mean it—his to give the law!
Detested spoiler!—his! a vile usurper!
Have we forgot the elder Dionysius,

Surnam'd the Tyrant? To Sicilia's throne
The monster waded thro' whole seas of blood.
Sore groan'd the land beneath his iron rod,
Till rous'd at length Evander came from Greece,
Like Freedom's Genius came, and sent the tyrant
Stript of the crown, and to his humble rank
Once more reduc'd, to roam, for vile subsistence,
A wandering sophist, thro' the realms of Greece.

    Phil. Melanthon, yes; full clearly I remember
The splendid day, when all rejoicing Sicily
Hail'd her deliverer.

    Melan. Shall the tyrant's son
Deduce a title from the father's guilt?
Philotas, thou wert once the friend of goodness;
Thou art a Greek; fair Corinth gave thee birth;
I mark'd thy growing youth; I need not tell,
With what an equal sway Evander reign'd,
How just, how upright, generous and good!
From ev'ry region bards and sages came;
Whate'er of science ancient Egypt stor'd,
All that the East had treasur'd; all that Greece
Of moral wisdom taught, and Plato's voice,
Was heard in Sicily. Shall Dionysius
Extinguish ev'ry virtue in the land,
Bow to his yoke the necks of freeborn men,
And here perpetuate a tyrant's reign?

    Phil. Whate'er his right, to him in Syracuse
All bend the knee; his the supreme dominion,
And death and torment wait his sovereign nod.

    Melan. But soon that pow'r shall cease: behold his walls
Now close encircled by the Grecian bands;
Timoleon leads them on; indignant Corinth
Sends her avenger forth, array'd in terror,
To hurl ambition from a throne usurp'd,
And bid all Sicily resume her rights.

    Phil.

Phil. Thou wert a statesman once, Melanthon; now,
Grown dim with age, thy eye pervades no more
The deep-laid schemes which Dionysius plans.
Know then, a fleet from Carthage even now
Stems the rough billow; and, e'er yonder sun,
That now declining seeks the Western wave,
Shall to the shades of night resign the world,
Thou'lt see the Punic sails in yonder bay,
Whose waters wash the walls of Syracuse.

Melan. Art thou a stranger to Timoleon's name?
Intent to plan, and circumspect to see
All possible events, he rushes on
Resistless in his course! Your boasted master
Scarce stands at bay; each hour the strong blockade
Hems him in closer, and ere long thou'lt view
Oppression's iron rod to fragments shiver'd!
The good Evander then———

Phil. Alas, Evander
Will ne'er behold the golden time you look for!

Melan. How! not behold it! Say, Philotas, speak;
Has the fell tyrant, have his felon murderers———

Phil. As yet, my friend, Evander lives.

Melan. And yet
Thy dark half-hinted purpose—Lead me to him—
If thou hast murder'd him———

Phil. By Heav'n, he lives.

Melan. Then bless me with one tender interview.
Thrice has the sun gone down, since last these eyes
Have seen the good old king; say, why is this?
Wherefore debar'd his presence? Thee, Philotas,
The troops obey, that guard the royal pris'ner;
Each avenue to thee is open; thou
Can'st grant admittance; let me, let me see him!

Phil. Entreat no more; the soul of Dionysius
Is ever wakeful; rent with all the pangs
That wait on conscious guilt.

Melan. But when dun night——
　Phil. Alas! it cannot be—But mark my words.
Let Greece urge on her general assault.
Dispatch some friend, who may o'er-leap the walls,
And tell Timoleon, the good old Evander
Has liv'd three days, by Dionysius' order,
Lock'd up from ev'ry sustenance of nature,
And life, now wearied out, almost expires.
　Melan. If any spark of virtue dwell within thee,
Lead me, Philotas, lead me to his prison.
　Phil. The tyrant's jealous care hath mov'd him thence.
　Melan. Ha! mov'd him, say'st thou?
　Phil. At the midnight hour,
Silent convey'd him up the steep ascent,
To where the elder Dionysius form'd,
On the sharp summit of the pointed rock,
Which overhangs the deep, a dungeon drear:
Cell within cell, a labyrinth of horror,
Deep cavern'd in the cliff, where many a wretch,
Unseen by mortal eye, has groan'd in anguish,
And died obscure, unpitied, and unknown.
　Melan. Clandestine murderer! Yes, there's the scene
Of horrid massacre. Full oft I've walk'd,
When all things lay in sleep and darkness hush'd.
Yes, oft I've walk'd the lonely sullen beach,
And heard the mournful sound of many a corse
Plung'd from the rock into the wave beneath,
That murmur'd on the shore. And means he thus
To end a monarch's life? Oh! grant my pray'r;
My timely succour may protect his days;
The guard is yours——
　Phil. Forbear; thou plead'st in vain;
I must not yield; it were assur'd destruction;
Farewell, dispatch a message to the Greeks;
I'll to my station; now thou know'st the worst. [*Exit.*
　　　　　　　　　　　　　　　　　　Melanthon.

MELANTHON.

Oh! lost Evander! Lost Euphrasia too!
How will her gentle nature bear the shock
Of a dear father, thus in ling'ring pangs
A prey to famine, like the verriest wretch
Whom the hard hand of Misery hath grip'd!
In vain she'll rave with impotence of sorrow;
Perhaps provoke her fate: Greece arms in vain;
All's lost; Evander dies!

Enter CALIPPUS.

Calip. Where is the king?
Our troops, that sallied to attack the foe,
Retire disordered; to the eastern gate
The Greeks pursue! Timoleon rides in blood!
Arm, arm, and meet their fury!
   Melan. To the citadel
Direct thy footsteps; Dionysius there
Marshals a chosen band.
   Calip. Do thou call forth
Thy hardy veterans; haste, or all is lost!   [*Exit.*
                                        [*Warlike music.*

MELANTHON.

Now, ye just Gods, now look propitious down;
Now give the Grecian sabre tenfold edge,
And save a virtuous king!
                                        [*Warlike music.*

Enter EUPHRASIA.

Euph. War on, ye heroes,
Ye great asserters of a monarch's cause!
Let the wild tempest rise. Melanthon, ha!
                                        Did'st

Did'st thou not hear the vast tremenduous roar?
Down tumbling from it's base the eastern tow'r,
Burst on the tyrant's ranks, and on the plain
Lies an extended ruin.

 Melan. Still new horrors
Increase each hour, and gather round our heads.

 Euph. The glorious tumult lifts my tow'ring soul.
Once more, Melanthon, once again, my father
Shall mount Sicilia's throne.

 Melan. Alas! that hour
Would come with joy to ev'ry honest heart,
Would shed divinest blessings from its wing;
But no such hour in all the round of time,
I fear, the Fates averse will e'er lead on.

 Euph. And still, Melanthon, still does pale Despair
Depress thy spirit? Lo! Timoleon comes
Arm'd with the pow'r of Greece; the brave, the just,
God-like Timoleon! ardent to redress,
He guides the war, and gains upon his prey.
A little interval shall set the victor
Within our gates triumphant.

 Melan. Still my fears,
Forbode for thee. Would thou hadst left this place,
When hence your husband, the brave Phocion fled,
Fled with your infant son!

 Euph. In duty fix'd,
Here I remain'd, while my brave gen'rous Phocion
Fled with my child, and from his mother's arms
Bore my sweet little one.—Full well thou know'st
The pangs I suffer'd in that trying moment;
Did I not weep? Did I not rave and shriek,
And by the roots tear my dishevell'd hair?
Did I not follow to the sea-beat shore,
Resolv'd with him and with my blooming boy
To trust the winds and waves?

          Melan.

Melan. Deem not, Euphrasia,
I e'er can doubt thy constancy and love.
　Euph. Melanthon, how I loved, the Gods who saw
Each secret image that my fancy form'd,
The Gods can witness how I lov'd my Phocion.
And yet I went not with him. Could I do it;
Could I desert my father? Could I leave
The venerable man, who gave me being,
A victim here in Syracuse, nor stay
To watch his fate, to visit his affliction,
To cheer his prison hours, and with the tear
Of filial virtue bid ev'n bondage smile?
　Melan. The pious act, whate'er the fates intend,
Shall merit heart-felt praise.
　Euph. Yes, Phocion, go,
Go with my child, torn from this matron breast,
This breast that still should yield it's nurture to him,
Fly with my infant to some happier shore.
If he be safe, Euphrasia dies content.
Till that sad close of all, the task be mine
To tend a father with delighted care,
To smooth the pillow of declining age,
See him sink gradual into mere decay,
On the last verge of life watch ev'ry look,
Explore each fond unutterable wish,
Catch his last breath, and close his eyes in peace.
　Melan. I would not add to my afflictions; yet
My heart misgives;—Evander's fatal period———
　Euph. Still is far off; the Gods have sent relief,
And once again I shall behold him king.
　Melan. Alas! this dream of hope at length may waken
To deep despair.
　Euph. The spirit-stirring virtue
That glows within me, ne'er shall know despair.
No, I will trust the Gods. Desponding man!

Hast thou not heard with what resistless ardour
Timoleon drives the tumult of the war?
Hast thou not heard him thund'ring at our gates?
The tyrant's pent up in his last retreat;
Anon thou'lt see his battlements in dust,
His walls, his ramparts, and his tow'rs in ruin;
Destruction pouring in on ev'ry side,
Pride and oppression at their utmost need,
And nought to save him in his hopeless hour.
      [*A flourish of trumpets.*

 Melan. Ha! the fell tyrant comes—Beguile his rage,
And o'er your sorrows cast a dawn of gladness.

  Enter DIONYSIUS, CALIPPUS, OFFICERS, &c.

 Di. The vain presumptuous Greek! His hopes of con-
Like a gay dream, are vanish'd into air.   [quest,
Proudly elate, and flush'd with easy triumph
O'er vulgar warriors, to the gates of Syracuse
He urg'd the war, till Dionysius' arm
Let slaughter loose, and taught his dastard train
To seek their safety by inglorious flight.

 Euph. O Dionysius, if distracting fears
Alarm this throbbing bosom, you will pardon
A frail and tender sex. Should ruthless war
Roam through our streets, and riot here in blood,
Where shall the lost Euphrasia find a shelter?
In vain she'll kneel, and clasp the sacred altar.
O let me then, in mercy let me seek
The gloomy mansion, where my father dwells;
I die content, if in his arms I perish.

 Dion. Thou lovely trembler, hush thy fears to rest.
The Greek recoils; like the impetuous surge
That dashes on the rock, there breaks, and foams,
And backward rolls into the sea again.
All shall be well in Syracuse: a fleet
          Appears

Appears in view, and brings the chosen sons
Of Carthage. From the hill that fronts the harbour,
I saw their canvas swelling with the wind,
While on the purple wave the western sun
Glanc'd the remains of day.

Euph. Yet till the fury
Of war subside, the wild, the horrid interval
In safety let me soothe to dear delight
In a lov'd father's presence; from his sight,
For three long days, with specious feign'd excuse
Your guards debarr'd me. Oh! while yet he lives,
Indulge a daughter's love; worn out with age
Soon must he seal his eyes in endless night,
And with his converse charm my ear no more.

Dion. Why thus anticipate misfortune? Still
Evander mocks the injuries of time.
Calippus, thou survey the city round;
Station the centinels, that no surprise
Invade the unguarded works, while drowsy night
Weighs down the soldier's eye. Afflicted fair,
Thy couch invites thee. When the tumult's o'er,
Thou'lt see Evander with redoubled joy.
Though now unequal to the cares of empire
His age sequester him, yet honours high
Shall gild the ev'ning of his various day.

Euph. For this benignity accept my thanks!
They gush in tears, and my heart pours it's tribute.

Dion. Perdiccas, ere the morn's revolving light
Unveil the face of things, do thou dispatch
A well-oar'd galley to Hamilcar's fleet;
At the north point of yonder promontory
Let some selected officer instruct him
To moor his ships, and issue on the land.
Then may Timoleon tremble: vengeance then
Shall overwhelm his camp, pursue his bands

With fatal havock to the ocean's margin,
And caſt their limbs to glut the vulture's famine
In mangled heaps upon the naked ſhore.
               [*Exit Dionyſius.*

EUPHRASIA, MELANTHON.

Euph. What do I hear? Melanthon, can it be?
If Carthage comes, if her perfidious ſons
Liſt in his cauſe, the dawn of freedom's gone.
   Melan. Woe, bitt'reſt woe impends; thou would'ſt not
   Euph. How!—ſpeak!—unfold.—   [think—
   Melan. My tongue denies it's office.
   Euph. How is my father? Say, Melanthon——
   Melan. He,———
Perhaps he dies this moment.—Since Timoleon
Firſt form'd his lines round this beleaguer'd city,
No nutriment has touch'd Evander's lips.
In the deep caverns of the rock impriſon'd
He pines in bittereſt want.
   Euph. To that abode
Of woe and horror, that laſt ſtage of life,
Has the fell tyrant mov'd him?
   Melan. There ſequeſter'd,
Alas! he ſoon muſt periſh.
   Euph. Well, my heart,
Well do your vital drops forget to flow.
   Melan. Enough his ſword has reek'd with public
         ſlaughter;
Now dark inſiduous deeds muſt thin mankind.
   Euph. Oh! night, that oft haſt heard my piercing
         ſhrieks
Diſturb thy awful ſilence; oft has heard
Each ſtroke theſe hands in frantic ſorrow gave
From this ſad breaſt reſounding, now no more
I mean to vent complaints; I mean not now

                              With

With busy mem'ry to retrace the wrongs
His hand hath heap'd on our devoted race.
I bear it all; with calmest patience bear it:
Resign'd and wretched, desperate and lost.

 Melan. Despair, alas! is all the sad resource
Our fate allows us now.

 Euph. Yet why despair?
Is that the tribute to a father due?
Blood is his due, Melanthon; yes, the blood,
The vile, black blood, that fills the tyrant's veins,
Would graceful look upon my dagger's point.
Come, vengeance, come, shake of this feeble sex,
Sinew my arm, and guide it to his heart.
And thou, O filial piety, that rul'st
My woman's breast, turn to vindicate rage;
Assume the port of justice; shew mankind
Tyrannic guilt hath never dar'd in Syracuse,
Beyond the reach of virtue.

 Melan. Yet beware;
Controul this frenzy that bears down your reason.
Surrounded by his guards, the tyrant mocks
Your utmost fury; moderate your zeal,
Nor let him hear these transports of the soul,
These wild upbraidings.

 Euph. Shall Euphrasia's voice
Be hush'd to silence, when a father dies;
Shall not the monster hear his deeds accurst?
Shall he not tremble, when a daughter comes,
Wild with her griefs, and terrible with wrongs,
Fierce in despair, all nature in her cause
Alarm'd and rouz'd to vengeance?—Yes, Melanthon,
The man of blood shall hear me; yes, my voice
Shall mount aloft upon the whirlwind's wing,
Pierce yon blue vault, and bring the thund'rer down.
Melanthon come; my wrongs will lend me force;

The

The weakness of my sex is gone; this arm
Feels tenfold strength; this arm shall do a deed
For Heav'n and earth, for men and Gods to wonder at:
This arm shall vindicate a father's cause.

END OF THE FIRST ACT.

ACT II.

A wild romantic Scene amidst overhanging Rocks; a Cavern on one Side.

ARCAS, *with a Spear in his Hand.*

THE gloom of night sits heavy on the world;
And o'er the solemn scene such stillness reigns,
As 'twere a pause of nature; on the beach
No murmuring billow breaks; the Grecian tents
Lie sunk in sleep; no gleaming fires are seen;
All Syracuse is hush'd; no stir abroad,
Save ever and anon the dashing oar,
That beats the sullen wave. And hark!—Was that
The groan of anguish from Evander's cell,
Piercing the midnight gloom?—It is the sound
Of bustling prows, that cleave the briny deep.
Perhaps at this dead hour Hamilcar's fleet
Rides in the bay.

Enter

Enter PHILOTAS, *from the Cavern.*

Phil. What ho!—brave Arcas!—ho!
Arcas. Why thus desert thy couch!
Phil. Methought the sound
Of distant uproar chas'd affrighted sleep.
  Arcas. At intervals the oar's resounding stroke
Comes ecchoing from the main. Save that report,
A death-like silence thro' the wide expanse
Broods o'er the dreary coast.
  Phil. Do thou retire,
And seek repose; the duty of thy watch
Is now perform'd; I take thy post.
  Arcas. How fares
Your royal pris'ner?
  Phil. Arcas, shall I own
A secret weakness? My heart inward melts
To see that suffering virtue. On the earth,
The cold, damp earth, the royal victim lies;
And while pale famine drinks his vital spirit,
He welcomes death, and smiles himself to rest.
Oh! would I could relieve him! Thou withdraw;
Thy wearied nature claims repose; and now
The watch is mine.
  Arcas. May no alarm disturb thee. [*Exit.*

PHILOTAS.

Some dread event is lab'ring into birth.
At close of day the sullen sky held forth
Unerring signals.—With disastrous glare
The moon's full orb rose crimson'd o'er with blood;
And lo! athwart the gloom a falling star
Trails a long tract of fire!——What daring step
Sounds on the flinty rock? Stand there; what ho!
Speak, ere thou dar'st advance.

Enter

Enter EUPHRASIA, *with a Lanthorn in her Hand.*

Euph. Thou need'ſt not fear;
It is a friend approaches.
　Phil. Ha! what mean
Thoſe plaintive notes?
　Euph. Here is no ambuſh'd Greek,
No warrior to ſurprize thee on the watch.
An humble ſuppliant comes—Alas my ſtrength
Exhauſted quite forſakes this weary frame.
　Phil. What voice thus piercing thro' the gloom of
　　　　night——
What art thou? Speak, unfold thy purpoſe; ſay,
What wretch, with what intent, at this dead hour—
Wherefore alarm'ſt thou thus our peaceful watch?
　Euph. Let no miſtruſt affright thee—Lo! a wretch,
The verieſt wretch that ever groan'd in anguiſh,
Comes here to grovel on the earth before thee,
To tell her ſad, ſad tale, implore thy aid,
For ſure the pow'r is thine, thou canſt relieve
My bleeding heart, and ſoften all my woes.
　Phil. Ha! ſure thoſe accents—*(takes the light from her.*
　Euph. Deign to liſten to me.
　Phil. Euphraſia!——
　Euph. Yes; the loſt, undone Euphraſia;
Supreme in wretchedneſs; to th' inmoſt ſenſe,
Here in the quickeſt fibre of the heart,
Wounded, transfix'd, and tortur'd to deſtraction.
　Phil. Why, princeſs, thus anticipate the dawn?
Still ſleep and ſilence wrap the weary world;
The ſtars in mid career uſurp the pole;
The Grecian bands, the winds, the waves are huſh'd;
All things are mute around us; all but you
Reſt in oblivious ſlumber from their cares.
　　　　　　　　　　　　　　　　　　Euph.

Euph. Yes; all at peace; I only wake to misery.
Phil. How didst thou gain the summit of the rock?
Euph. Give me my father; here you hold him fetter'd;
Oh! give him to me;—in the fond pursuit
All pain and peril vanish; love and duty
Inspir'd the thought; despair itself gave courage;
I climb'd the hard ascent; with painful toil
Surmounted craggy cliffs, and pointed rocks;
What will not misery attempt?—If ever
The touch of nature throbb'd within your breast,
Admit me to Evander; in these caves
I know he pines in want; let me convey
Some charitable succour to a father.
Phil. Alas! Euphrasia, would I dare comply.
Euph. It will be virtue in thee. Thou, like me,
Wert born in Greece:—Oh! by our common parent.—
Nay stay; thou shalt not fly; Philotas stay—
You have a father too;—think were his lot
Hard as Evander's if, by felon hands
Chain'd to the earth, with slow consuming pangs
He felt sharp want, and with an asking eye
Implor'd relief, yet cruel men deny'd it,
Would'st thou not burst thro' adamantine gates,
Thro' walls and rocks, to save him? Think, Philotas,
Of thy own aged sire, and pity mine.
Think of the agonies a daughter feels,
When thus a parent wants the common food,
The bounteous hand of nature meant for all.
Phil. 'Twere best withdraw thee, princess; thy assistance
Evander wants not; it is fruitless all;
Thy tears, thy wild entreaties, are in vain.
Euph. Ha!—thou hast murder'd him; he is no more;
I understand thee;—butchers, you have shed
The precious drops of life; yet, e'en in death,
Let me behold him; let a daughter close

D   With

With duteous hand a father's beamless eyes;
Print her last kisses on his honour'd hand,
And lay him decent in the shroud of death.

   Phil. Alas! this frantic grief can nought avail.
Retire, and seek the couch of balmy sleep,
In this dead hour, this season of repose.

   Euph. And dost thou then, inhuman that thou art,
Advise a wretch like me to know repose?
This is my last abode: these caves, these rocks,
Shall ring for ever with Euphrasia's wrongs;
All Sicily shall hear me; yonder deep
Shall echo back an injur'd daughter's cause;
Here will I dwell, and rave, and shriek, and give
These scatter'd locks to all the passing winds;
Call on Evander lost; and, pouring curses,
And cruel gods, and cruel stars invoking,
Stand on the cliff in madness and despair.

   Phil. Yet calm this violence; reflect, Euphrasia,
With what severe enforcement Dionysius
Exacts obedience to his dread command.
If here thou'rt found——

   Euph. Here is Euphrasia's mansion, *(falls on the ground.)*
Her fix'd eternal home;—inhuman savages,
Here stretch me with a father's murder'd corse;
Then heap your rocks, your mountains on my head;
It will be kindness in you; I shall rest
Intomb'd within a parent's arms.

   Phil. By Heav'n,
My heart in pity bleeds.

   Euph. Talk'st thou of pity?
Yield to the gen'rous instinct; grant my pray'r;
Let my eyes view him, gaze their last upon him,
And shew you have some sense of human woe.

   Phil. Her vehemence of grief o'erpow'rs me quite.
My honest heart condemns the barb'rous deed,
And if I dare——   *Euph.*

Euph. And if you dare!——Is that
The voice of manhood? Honest, if you dare!
'Tis the slave's virtue! 'tis the utmost limit
Of the base coward's honour.——Not a wretch,
There's not a villain, not a tool of pow'r,
But, silence interest, extinguish fear,
And he will prove benevolent to man.
The gen'rous heart does more; will dare to all
That honour prompts.—How dost thou dare to murder?—
Respect the gods, and know no other fear.

Phil. Oh! thou hast conquer'd.—Yes, Euphrasia, go
Behold thy father——

Euph. Raise me, raise me up;
I'll bathe thy hand with tears, thou gen'rous man!

Phil. Yet mark my words; if aught of nourishment
Thou would'st convey, my partners of the watch
Will ne'er consent——

Euph. I will observe your orders:
On any terms, oh! let me, let me see him.

Phil. Yon lamp will guide thee thro' the cavern'd way.

Euph. My heart runs o'er in thanks; the pious act
Timoleon shall reward; the bounteous gods,
And thy own virtue shall reward the deed.
(Goes into the cave.

PHILOTAS.

Prevailing, pow'rful virtue!—Thou subdu'st
The stubborn heart, and mould'st it to thy purpose.
Would I could save them!—But tho' not for me
The glorious pow'r to shelter innocence,
Yet for a moment to assuage its woes,
Is the best sympathy, the purest joy
Nature intended for the heart of man,
When thus she gave the social gen'rous tear. [*Exit.*

Scene the Inside of the Cavern.

Enter ARCAS *and* EUPHRASIA.

Arcas. No; on my life I dare not.
Euph. But a small,
A wretched pittance; one poor cordial drop
To renovate exhausted drooping age,
I ask no more.
Arcas. Not the smallest store
Of scanty nourishment must pass these walls.
Our lives were forfeit else: a moment's parley
Is all I grant; in yonder cave he lies.
Evander (within the cell.) Oh! struggling nature! let
thy conflict end.
Oh! give me, give me rest.
Euph. My father's voice!
It pierces here! it cleaves my very heart.
I shall expire, and never see him more.
Arcas. Repose thee, princess, here, *(draws a couch.)*
here rest thy limbs,
Till the returning blood shall lend thee firmness.
Euph. The caves, the rocks, re-echo to his groans,
And is there no relief?
Arcas. All I can grant
You shall command.—I will unbar the dungeon,
Unloose the chain that binds him to the rock,
And leave your interview without restraint.
[*Opens a cell in the back Scene.*]
Euph. Hold, hold my heart! Oh! how shall I sustain
The agonizing scene? *(rises.)* I must behold him;
Nature, that drives me on, will lend me force.
Is that his mansion?
Arcas.

Arcas. Take your laſt farewell.
His vigour ſeems not yet exhauſted quite.
You muſt be brief, or ruin will enſue.　　　[*Exit.*
　Evan. (*raiſing himſelf.*) Oh! when ſhall I get free?——
　　Theſe ling'ring pangs———
　Euph. Behold ye pow'rs, that ſpectacle of woe!
　Evan. Diſpatch me, pitying gods, and ſave my child!
I burn, I burn; alas! no place of reſt: [*Riſes and comes out.*
A little air; once more a breath of air;
Alas! I faint; I die.
　Euph. Heart-piercing ſight!
Let me ſupport you, Sir,
　Evan. Oh! lend your arm,———
Whoe'er thou art, I thank thee———That kind breeze
Comes gently o'er my ſenſes———Lead me forward——
And is there left one charitable hand
To reach it's ſuccour to a wretch like me?
　Euph. Well may'ſt thou aſk it. Oh! my breaking heart!
The hand of death is on him.
　Evan. Still a little,
A little onward to the air conduct me;
'Tis well;—I thank thee; thou art kind and good,
And much I wonder at this gen'rous pity.
　Euph. Do you not know me, Sir?
　Evan. Methinks I know
That voice——— art thou———alas! my eyes are dim!
Each object ſwims before me———No, in truth
I do not know thee.———
　Euph. Not your own Euphraſia?
　Evan. Art thou my daughter?
　Euph. Oh! my honour'd Sire!
　Evan. My daughter, my Euphraſia? come to cloſe
A father's eyes!———Giv'n to my laſt embrace!
Gods! do I hold her once again?———Your mercies
Are without number———[*falls on the couch.*]
　　　　　　　　　　　　　　　　　　This

This excess of bliss
O'erpow'rs—it kills—Euphrasia—could I hope it?
I die content——Art thou indeed my daughter?
Thou art—my hand is moisten'd with thy tears——
I pray you do not weep—thou art my child—
I thank you gods?—in my last dying moments
You have not left me—I would pour my praise——
You read my heart—you see what passes there.

  Euph. Alas he faints; the gushing tide of transport
Bears down each feeble sense——Restore him Heaven!

  Evan. All, my Euphrasia, all will soon be well.
Pass but a moment, and this busy globe,
Its thrones, its empires, and its bustling millions,
Will seem a speck in the great void of space.
Yet while I stay, thou darling of my age—
Nay dry those tears—

  Euph. I will my father.

  Evan. Where,
I fear to ask it, where is virtuous Phocion?

  Euph. Fled from the tyrant's pow'r.

  Evan. And left thee here
Expos'd and helpless?

  Euph. He is all truth and honour:
He fled to save my child.

  Evan. My young Evander!
Your boy is safe Euphrasia?—Oh! my heart—
Alas! quite gone; worn out with misery;
Oh! weak, decay'd old man!

  Euph. Inhuman wretches!
Will none relieve his want?—A drop of water
Might save his life; and ev'n that's deny'd him.

  Evan. These strong emotions—Oh! that eager air—
It is too much—Assist me; bear me hence;
And lay me down in peace.

  Euph. His eyes are fix'd!

                                    And

And thofe pale quiv'ring lips!—He clafps my hand—
What, no affiftance!—Monfters will you thus
Let him expire in thefe weak feeble arms?

Enter PHILOTAS.

Phil. Thofe wild, thofe piercing fhrieks will give th'
   alarm.
Euph. Support him; bear him hence; 'tis all I afk.
Evan. (*As he is carried off.*) O Death! where art thou?
   ———Death, thou dread of guilt,
Thou wifh of innocence, affliction's friend,
Tir'd nature calls thee—Come, in mercy come,
And lay me pillow'd in eternal reft.
My child—where art thou? Give me—reach thy hand—
Why doft thou weep?—My eyes are dry—Alas!
Quite parch'd—my lips—quite parch'd—they cling—
   together.
Euph. Now judge, ye Pow'rs, in the whole round
   of time,
If e'er you view'd a fcene of woe like this. [*Exeunt.*

Enter ARCAS.

Arcas. The grey of morn breaks thro' yon eaftern clouds.
'Twere time this interview fhould end; the hour
Now warns Euphrafia hence; what man could dare,
I have indulg'd—Philotas!—ha! the cell
Left void!—Evander gone!—What may this mean?
Philotas, fpeak.

Enter PHILOTAS.

Phil. Oh! vile, detefted lot
Here to obey the favage tyrant's will,
And murder virtue, that can thus behold

                                    It's

It's executioner, and smile upon him.
That piteous sight!

Arcas. She must withdraw Philotas;
Delay undoes us both. The restless main
Glows with the blush of day. Timoleon's fleet,
That pass'd the night in busy preparation,
Makes from the shore. On the high craggy point
Of yonder jutting eminence I mark'd
Their haughty streamers curling to the wind.
He seeks Hamilcar's fleet. The briny deep
Shall soon be dy'd with blood. The fierce alarm
Will rouze our slumb'ring troops. The time requires
Without or further pause, or vain excuse,
That she depart this moment.

Phil. Arcas, yes;
My voice shall warn her of th' approaching danger. [*Exit.*

Arcas. Would she had ne'er adventur'd to our guard.
I dread th' event; and hark!—the wind conveys
In clearer sound the uproar of the main.
The fates prepare new havock; on th' event
Depends the fate of empire. Wherefore thus
Delays Euphrasia?—Ha! what means, Philotas,
That sudden haste, that pale disorder'd look?

Enter PHILOTAS.

Phil. O! I can hold no more; at such a sight
Ev'n the hard heart of tyranny would melt
To infant softness. Arcas, go, behold
The pious fraud of charity and love;
Behold that unexampled goodness; see
Th' expedient sharp necessity has taught her;
Thy heart will burn, will melt, will yearn to view,
A child like her.

Arcas. Ha!—Say what mystery
Wakes these emotions?

Phil.

Phil. Wonder-working virtue!
The father foster'd at his daughter's breast!—
O! filial piety!—The milk design'd
For her own offspring, on the parent's lip
Allays the parching fever.

Arcas. That device
Has she then form'd, eluding all our care,
To minister relief?

Phil. On the bare earth
Evander lies; and as his languid pow'rs
Imbibe with eager thirst the kind refreshment,
And his looks speak unutterable thanks,
Euphrasia views him with the ten'drest glance,
Ev'n as a mother doating on her child,
And, ever and anon, amidst the smiles
Of pure delight, of exquisite sensation,
A silent tear steals down; the tear of virtue,
That sweetens grief to rapture. All her laws
Inverted quite, great Nature triumphs still.

Arcas. The tale unmans my soul.

Phil. Ye tyrants hear it,
And learn, that, while your cruelty prepares
Unheard of torture, virtue can keep pace
With your worst efforts, and can try new modes
To bid men grow enamour'd of her charms.

Arcas. Philotas, for Euphrasia, in her cause
I now can hazard all. Let us preserve
Her father for her.

Phil. Oh! her lovely daring
Transcends all praise. By Heav'n, he shall not die.

Arcas. And yet we must be wary; I'll go forth,
And first explore each avenue around,
Lest the fix'd sentinel obstruct your purpose. [*Exit.*

Phil. I thank thee, Arcas; we will act like men

E   Who

Who feel another's woes—She leads him forth,
And tremblingly supports his drooping age.
[*Goes to assist him.*

Enter EUPHRASIA, *and* EVANDER.

Evan. Euphrasia, oh! my child! returning life
Glows here about my heart. Conduct me forward—
At the last gasp preserv'd! Ha! dawning light!
Let me behold; in faith I see thee now;
I do indeed: the father sees his child.

Euph. I have reliev'd him—Oh! the joy's too great;
'Tis speechless rapture!

Evan. Blessings, blessings on thee!

Euph. My father still shall live. Alas! Philotas,
Could I abandon that white hoary head,
That venerable form?—Abandon him
To perish here in misery and famine?

Phil. Thy tears, thou miracle of goodness!
Have triumph'd o'er me; these round gushing drops
Attest your conquest. Take him, take your father;
Convey him hence; I do release him to you.

Evan. What said Philotas!—Do I fondly dream?
Indeed my senses are imperfect; yet
Methought I heard him! Did he say release me?

Phil. Thou art my king, and now no more my pris'ner;
Go with your daughter, with that wond'rous pattern
Of filial piety to after times.
Yes, princess, lead him forth; I'll point the path,
Whose soft declivity will guide your steps
To the deep vale, which these o'erhanging rocks
Encompass round. You may convey him thence
To some safe shelter. Yet a moment's pause;
I must conceal your flight from ev'ry eye.
Yes, I will save 'em—Oh! returning virtue!
How big with joy one moment in thy service!
That wretched pair! I'll perish in their cause. [*Exit.*

EUPHRASIA,

EUPHRASIA, EVANDER.

Evan. Whither, oh! whither shall Evander go?
I'm at the goal of life; if in the race
Honour has follow'd with no ling'ring step,
But there sits smiling with her laurel'd wreath,
To crown my brow, there would I fain make halt,
And not inglorious lay me down to rest.

Euph. And will you then refuse, when thus the Gods
Afford a refuge to thee?

Evan. Oh! my child,
There is no refuge for me.

Euph. Pardon, Sir:
Euphrasia's care has form'd a safe retreat;
There may'st thou dwell; it will not long be wanted;
Soon shall Timoleon, with resistless force,
Burst yon devoted walls.

Evan. Timoleon!

Euph. Yes,
The brave Timoleon, with the pow'r of Greece;
Another day shall make the city his.

Evan. Timoleon come to vindicate my rights!
Oh! thou shall reign in Sicily!—My child
Shall grace her father's throne. Indulgent Heav'n!
Pour down your blessings on this best of daughters;
To her and Phocion give Evander's crown;
Let them, oh! let them both in virtue wear it,
And in due time transmit it to their boy!

Enter PHILOTAS.

Phil. All things are apt;—the drowsy sentinel
Lies hush'd in sleep; I'll marshal thee the way
Down the steep rock.

Euph. Oh! Let us quickly hence.

Evan. The blood but loiters in these frozen veins.
Do you, whose youthful spirit glows with life,
Do you go forth, and leave this mould'ring corpse.

To me had Heav'n decree'd a longer date,
It ne'er had suffer'd a fell monster's reign,
Nor let me see the carnage of my people.
Farewell, Euphrasia; in one lov'd embrace
To these remains pay the last obsequies,
And leave me here to sink to silent dust.

Euph. And will you then, on self-destruction bent,
Reject my pray'r, nor trust your fate with me?

Evan. Trust thee! Euphrasia? Trust in thee my child?
Tho' life's a burden I could well lay down,
Yet I will prize it, since bestow'd by thee.
Oh! thou art good; thy virtue soars a flight
For the wide world to wonder at; in thee,
Hear it all nature, future ages hear it,
The father finds a parent in his child.

END of the SECOND ACT.

ACT III.

Scene a Rampart near the Harbour.

Enter MELANTHON *and* PHILOTAS.

Melan. AND lives he still?
Phil. He does; and kindly aliment
Renews the springs of life.
Melan. And doth he know
The glorious work the destinies prepare?
Phil. He is inform'd of all.
Melan. That Greek Timoleon
Comes his deliverer, and the fell usurper
Pants in the last extreme?
Phil. The glorious tidings
Have reach'd his ear.
Melan. Lead on, propitious Pow'r,
Your great design; second the Grecian arms,
And whelm the sons of Carthage in the deep.
Phil. This hour decides their doom; and, lo! Euphrasia
Stands on the jutting rock, that rock, where oft
Whole days she sat in pensive sorrow fix'd,
And swell'd with streaming tears the restless deep.
There, now with other sentiments elate,
She views Timoleon with victorious prow
Glide thro' the waves, and sees the scatter'd navy
Of Carthage fly before him.
Melan. Blest event!
Evander, if thou mock'st me not, shall live
Once more to see the justice of the Gods.
But wilt thou still protect my royal master?
Wilt thou admit me to his wish'd-for presence?

Phil.

Phil. Let it suffice that no assassin's aim
Can now assault him—I must hence, Melanthon;
I now must mingle with the tyrant's train,
And, with a semblance of obsequious duty,
Delude suspicion's eye—My friend, farewel.　　[*Exit.*

　　　MELANTHON.
If he deceive me not with specious hopes,
I shall behold the sov'reign, in whose service
These temples felt the iron casque of war,
And these white hairs have silver'd o'er my head.

　　Enter EUPHRASIA.
Euph. See there; behold 'em; lo! the fierce encounter;
He rushes on; the ocean flames around
With the bright flash of arms; the echoing hills,
Rebellow to the roar.
　Melan. The Gods are with us,
And victory is ours.
　Euph. High on the stern
The Grecian leaders stand: they stem the surge,
Launch'd from their arm the missive lightnings fly,
And the Barbaric fleet is wrapt in fire.
And lo! yon bark, down in the roaring gulph;
And there, more, more are perishing—Behold!
They plunge for ever lost.
　Melan. So perish all,
Who from yon continent unfurl'd their sails,
To shake the freedom of this sea-girt isle!
　Euph. Did I not say, Melanthon, did I not
Presage the glories of Timoleon's triumph!
Where now are Afric's sons? The vanquish'd tyrant
Shall look aghast; his heart shall shrink appall'd,
And dread his malefactions! Worse than famine,
Despair shall fasten on him!—
　　　　　　　　　　　　　　　Enter

Enter DIONYSIUS, CALIPPUS, &c.

Dion. Base deserters!
Curse on their Punic faith! Did they once dare
To grapple with the Greek? Ere yet the main
Was ting'd with blood, they turn'd their ships averse.
May storms and tempests follow in their rear,
And dash their fleet upon the Lybian shore!

Enter CALIPPUS.

Calip. My liege, Timoleon where the harbour opens
Has storm'd the forts, and ev'n now his fleet
Pursues its course, and steers athwart the bay.
  Dion. Ruin impends; and yet, if fall it must,
I bear a mind to meet it, undismay'd,
Unconquer'd ev'n by Fate.
  Calip. Through ev'ry street
Despair and terror fly. A panic spreads
From man to man, and superstition sees
Jove arm'd with thunder, and the Gods against us.
  Dion. With sacred rites their wrath must be appeas'd.
Let instant victims at the altar bleed;
Let incense roll its fragrant clouds to Heav'n,
And pious matrons, and the virgin train,
In slow procession to the temple bear
The image of their Gods.
  Euph. Ha!—Does the tyrant
Dare with unhallow'd step, with crimes and guilt,
Approach the sacred fane?—Alas! my father,
Where now thy sanctuary?—What place shall hide
Thy persecuted virtue? (*Aside.*)
  Dion. Thou, Euphrasia,
Lead forth the pious band.——This very moment
Issue our orders.

Euph.

Euph. With consenting heart
Euphrasia goes to waft her pray'rs to Heav'n. [*Exit.*
　Dion. The solemn sacrifice, the virgin throng,
Will gain the popular belief, and kindle
In the fierce soldiery religious rage.
Away, my friends, prepare the solemn pomp.
　　　　　　　　　　　[*Exit* CALIPPUS, *&c.*
Philotas, thou draw near: how fares your prisoner?
Has he yet breath'd his last?
　Phil. Life ebbs apace;
Tomorrow's sun sees him a breathless corse.
　Dion. Curse on his ling'ring pangs! Sicilia's crown
No more shall deck his brow; and if the sand
Still loiter in the glass, thy hand, my friend,
May shake it thence.
　Phil. It shall, dread Sir; that task
Leave to thy faithful servant.
　Dion. Oh! Philotas,
Thou little know'st the cares, the pangs of empire.
The ermin'd pride, the purple that adorns
A conqueror's breast, but serves, my friend, to hide
A heart that's torn, that's mangled with remorse.
Each object round me wakens horrid doubts;
The flatt'ring train, the centinel that guards me,
The slave that waits, all give some new alarm,
And from the means of safety dangers rise.
Ev'n victory itself plants anguish here,
And round my laurels the fell serpent twines.
　Phil. Would Dionysius abdicate his crown,
And sue for terms of peace?
　Dion. Detested thought!
No, though ambition teems with countless ills,
It still has charms of pow'r to fire the soul.
Tho' horrors multiply around my head,
I will oppose them all. The pomp of sacrifice
　　　　　　　　　　　　　　　　　　But

But now ordain'd, is mockery to Heav'n.
'Tis vain, 'tis fruitless; then let daring guilt
Be my inspirer, and consummate all.
Where are those Greeks, the captives of my sword,
Whose desp'rate valour rush'd within our walls,
Fought near our person, and the pointed lance
Aim'd at my breast?

   Phil. In chains they wait their doom.

   Dion. Give me to see 'em; bring the slaves before me.

   Phil. What, ho! Melanthon, this way lead your pri-
soners.

Enter MELANTHON *with Greek Officers and Soldiers.*

   Dion. Assassins and not warriors! do ye come,
When the wide range of battle claims your sword,
Thus do you come against a single life
To wage the war? Did not our buckler ring
With all your darts in one collected volley
Shower'd on my head? Did not your swords at once
Point at my breast, and thirst for regal blood?

   Greek Of. We sought thy life. I am by birth a Greek,
An open foe in arms I meant to slay
The foe of human kind.—With rival ardour
We took the field; one voice, one mind, one heart;
All leagu'd, all covenanted: in yon camp
Spirits there are who aim, like us, at glory.
Whene'er you sally forth, whene'er the Greeks
Shall scale your walls, prepare thee to encounter
A like assault. By me the youth of Greece
Thus notify the war they mean to wage.

   Dion. Thus then I warn them of my great revenge,
Whoe'er in battle shall become our pris'ner,
In torment meets his doom.

   Greek Of. Then wilt thou see,
How vile the body to a mind that pants

For genuine glory. Twice three hundred Greeks
Have sworn, like us, to hunt thee through the ranks;
Ours the first lot; we've fail'd; on yonder plain
Appear in arms, the faithful band will meet thee.

  Dion. Vile slave, no more. Melanthon drag 'em hence
To die in misery. Impal'd alive
The winds shall parch them on the craggy cliff.
Selected from the rest let one depart
A messenger to Greece, to tell the fate
Her chosen sons, her first adventurers, met.   [*Exit.*

  Melar. Unhappy men! how shall my care protect
Your forfeit lives?—Philotas, thou conduct them
To the deep dungeon's gloom. In that recess,
Midst the wild tumult of eventful war,
We may ward off the blow. My friends, farewel:
That officer will guide your steps.
            [*All follow* PHILOTAS, *except* PHOCION.

  Pho. Disguis'd
Thus in a soldier's garb he knows me not.
Melanthon!———

  Melan. Ha!—Those accents!—Phocion here?

  Pho. Yes, Phocion here! Speak, quickly tell me, say
How fares Euphrasia?

  Melan. Ha! beware;———Philotas,
Conduct these pris'ners hence; this soldier here
Shall bear the tidings to Timoleon's camp.

  Pho. Oh! satisfy my doubts; how fares Euphrasia?

  Melan. Euphrasia lives, and fills the anxious moments
With ev'ry virtue.—Wherefore venture hither?
Why with rash valour penetrate our gates?

  Pho. Could I refrain? Oh! could I tamely wait
Th' event of ling'ring war? With patience count
The lazy-pacing hours, while here in Syracuse
The tyrant keeps all that my heart holds dear?
For her dear sake, all danger sinks before me;

For her I burſt the barriers of the gate,
Where the deep cavern'd rock affords a paſſage.
A hundred choſen Greeks purſu'd my ſteps,
We forc'd an entrance; the devoted guard
Fell victims to our rage; but in that moment
Down from the walls ſuperior numbers came.
The tyrant led them on. We ruſh'd upon him,
If we could reach his heart, to end the war.
But Heav'n thought otherwiſe. Melanthon, ſay,
I fear to aſk it, lives Evander ſtill?

Melan. Alas, he lives impriſon'd in the rock.
Thou muſt withdraw thee hence; regain once more
Timoleon's camp; alarm his ſlumb'ring rage:
Aſſail the walls; thou with thy plalanx ſeek
The ſubterraneous path; that way at night
The Greeks may enter, and let in deſtruction
To the great work of vengeance.

Pho. Would'ſt thou have me
Baſely retreat, while my Euphraſia trembles
Here on the ridge of peril? She perhaps
May fall unknown, unpitied, undiſtinguiſh'd
Amidſt the gen'ral carnage. Shall I leave her
To add that beauty to the purple heap?
No; I will ſeek her in theſe walls accurſt,
Ev'n in the tyrant's palace; ſave that life,
My only ſource of joy, that life, whoſe loſs
Would make all Greece complotter in a murder,
And damn a righteous cauſe.

Melan. Yet hear the voice
Of ſober age. Should Dionyſius' ſpies
Detect thee here, ruin involves us all;
'Twere beſt retire, and ſeek Timoleon's tents;
Tell him, diſmay and terror fill the city;
Ev'n now in Syracuſe the tyrant's will
Ordains with pomp oblations to the Gods,

His deadly hand still hot with recent blood,
The monster dares approach the sacred altar;
Thy voice may rouse Timoleon to th' assault,
And bid him storm the works.

   Pho. By Heav'n I will;
My breath shall wake his rage; this very night,
When sleep sits heavy on the slumb'ring city,
Then Greece unsheaths her sword, and great revenge
Shall stalk with death and horror o'er the ranks
Of slaughter'd troops, a sacrifice to freedom!
But first let me behold Euphrasia.

   Melan. Hush
Thy pent-up valour; to a secret haunt
I'll guide thy steps; there dwell, and in apt time
I'll bring Euphrasia to thy longing arms.

   Pho. Wilt thou?

   Melan. By Heav'n I will; another act
Of desperate fury might endanger all.
The tyrant's busy guards are posted round;
In silence follow; thou shalt see Euphrasia.

   Pho. Oh! lead me to her; that exalted virtue
With firmer nerve shall bid me grasp the javelin,
Shall bid my sword with more than lightning's swiftness
Blaze in the front of war, and glut its rage
With blow repeated in the tyrant's veins.   [*Exeunt.*

Scene a Temple, with a Monument in the Middle.

Enter EUPHRASIA, ERIXENE, *and other Female Attendants.*

   Euph. This way, my virgins, this way bend your steps.
Lo! the sad sepulchre where, hears'd in death,
The pale remains of my dear mother lie.
There, while the victims at yon altar bleed,
                                       And

And with your pray'rs the vaulted roof refounds,
There let me pay the tribute of a tear,
A weeping pilgrim o'er Eudocia's ashes.
  Erix. Forbear, Euphrafia, to renew your forrows.
  Euph. My tears have dry'd their fource; then let me here
Pay this fad vifit to the honour'd clay
That moulders in the tomb.   Thefe facred viands
I'll burn an off'ring to a parent's fhade,
And fprinkle with this wine the hallow'd mould,
That duty paid, I will return, my virgins.
                    [*She goes into the tomb.*
  Erix. Look down, propitious Pow'rs! behold that virtue,
And heal the pangs that defolate her foul.

               Enter PHILOTAS.

  Phil. Mourn, mourn, ye virgins; rend your fcatter'd
        garments;
Some dread calamity hangs o'er our heads.
In vain the tyrant would appeafe with facrifice
Th' impending wrath of ill-requited Heav'n.
Ill omens hover o'er us: at the altar
The victim dropt, ere the divining feer
Had gor'd his knife. The brazen ftatues trembled,
And from the marble, drops of blood diftill'd.
  Erix. Now, ye juft Gods, if vengeance you prepare,
Now find the guilty head.
  Phil. Amidft the throng
A matron labours with th' infpiring God;
She ftares, fhe raves, and with no mortal found
Proclaims aloud, "Where Phœbus am I borne?
" I fee their glitt'ring fpears; I fee them charge;
" Bellona wades in blood; that mangled body,
" Deform'd with wounds and welt'ring in its gore,
" I know it well; Oh! clofe the dreadful fcene;
" Relieve me Phœbus, I have feen too much."
                                      Erix.

Erix. Alas! I tremble for Evander's fate;
Avert the omen, Gods, and guard his life.

Enter EUPHRASIA *from the Tomb.*

Euph. Virgins, I thank you—Oh! more lightly now
My heart expands; the pious act is done,
And I have paid my tribute to a parent.
Ah! wherefore does the tyrant bend his way?
　Phil. He flies the altar; leaves th' unfinish'd rites.
No God there smiles propitious on his cause,
Fate lifts the awful balance; weighs his life,
The lives of numbers, in the trembling scale.
　Euph. Despair and horror mark his haggard looks,
His wild, disorder'd step—He rushes forth;
Some new alarm demands him!—Ev'n now
He issues at yon portal!—Lo! see there,
The suppliant crowd disperses; wild with fear,
Distraction in each look, the wretched throng
Pours thro' the brazen gates—Do you retire,
Retire Philotas; let me here remain,
And give the moments of suspended fate
To pious worship and to filial love.
　Phil. Alas! I fear to yield:—awhile I'll leave thee,
And at the temple's entrance wait thy coming. [*Exit.*
　Euph. Now then, Euphrasia, now thou may'st indulge
The purest ecstacy of soul. Come forth,
Thou man of woe, thou man of ev'ry virtue.

Enter EVANDER *from the Monument.*

Evan. And does the grave thus cast me up again
With a fond father's love to view thee? Thus
To mingle rapture in a daughter's arms?
　Euph. How fares my father now?

Evan.

Evan. Thy aid, Euphrasia,
Has giv'n new life. Thou from this vital stream
Deriv'st thy being; with unheard-of duty
Thou hast repaid it to thy native source.
  Euph. Sprung from Evander, if a little portion
Of all his goodness dwell within my heart,
Thou wilt not wonder.
  Evan. Joy and wonder rise
In mix'd emotions!—Though departing hence,
After the storms of a tempestuous life,
Tho' I was entering the wish'd-for port,
Where all is peace, all bliss, and endless joy,
Yet here contented I can linger still
To view thy goodness, and applaud thy deeds,
Thou author of my life!—Did ever parent
Thus call his child before?—My heart's too full,
My old fond heart runs o'er; it akes with joy.
  Euph. Alas, too much you over-rate your daughter;
Nature and duty call'd me—Oh! my father,
How didst thou bear thy long, long suff'rings? How
Endure their barb'rous rage?
  Evan. My foes but did
To this old frame, what Nature's hand must do.
In the worst hour of pain, a voice still whisper'd me,
" Rouze thee, Evander; self-acquitting conscience
" Declares thee blameless, and the gods behold thee."
I was but going hence by mere decay
To that futurity which Plato taught,
Where the immortal spirit views the planets
Roll round the mighty year, and wrapt in bliss
Adores th' ideas of th' eternal mind.
Thither, oh! thither was Evander going,
But thou recall'st me; thou!—
  Euph. Timoleon too
Invites thee back to life.

Evan.

Evan. And does he still
Urge on the siege?
   Euph. His active genius comes
To scourge a guilty race. The Punic fleet
Half lost is swallow'd by the roaring sea.
The shatter'd refuse seek the Lybian shore,
To bear the news of their defeat to Carthage.
   Evan. These are thy wonders heaven!—Abroad thy
     spirit
Moves o'er the deep, and mighty fleets are vanish'd.
   Euph. Ha!—hark!—what noise is that! It comes
     this way.
Some busy footstep beats the hallow'd pavement.
Oh! Sir, retire—Ye Pow'rs!—Philotas!—ha!

     Enter PHILOTAS.

   Phil. For thee, Euphrasia, Dionysius calls:
Some new suspicion goads him. At yon gate
I stopt Calippus, as with eager haste
He bent this way to seek thee.—Oh! my sovereign,
My king, my injur'd master, will you pardon
The wrongs I've done thee?   (*kneels to Evander.*)
   Evan. Virtue such as thine,
From the fierce trial of tyrannic pow'r,
Shines forth with added lustre.
   Phil. Oh! forgive
My ardent zeal—there is no time to waste.
You must withdraw—Trust to your faithful friends.
Pass but another day, and Dionysius
Falls from a throne usurp'd.
   Evan. But ere he pays
The forfeit of his crimes, what streams of blood
Shall flow in torrents round! Methinks I might
Prevent this waste of nature—I'll go forth,
And to my people shew their rightful king.
                                      Euph.

Euph. Banish that thought; forbear; the rash attempt
Were fatal to our hopes; opprefs'd, difmay'd,
The people look aghaft, and wan with fear
None will efpoufe your caufe.

Evan. Yes all will dare
To act like men;—their king, I gave myfelf
To a whole people. I made no referve;
My life was their's; each drop about my heart
Pledg'd to the public caufe; devoted to it;
That was my compact; is the fubject's lefs?
If they are all debas'd, and willing flaves,
The young but breathing to grow grey in bondage,
And the old finking to ignoble graves,
Of fuch a race no matter who is king.
And yet I will not think it; no! my people
Are brave and gen'rous; I will truft their valour. [*going.*

Euph. Yet ftay; yet be advis'd.

Phil. As yet my liege,
No plan is fix'd, and no concerted meafure.
The fates are bufy: wait the vaft event.
Truft to my truth and honour. Witnefs, Gods.
Here in the temple of Olympian Jove
Philotas fwears——

Evan. Forbear: the man like thee,
Who feels the beft emotions of the heart,
Truth, reafon, juftice, honour's fine excitements,
Acts by thofe laws, and wants no other fanction.

Euph. Again, th' alarm approaches; fure deftruction
To thee, to all will follow:—hark! a found
Comes hollow murmuring thro' the vaulted ifle.
It gains upon the ear.——Withdraw, my father;
All's loft if thou art feen.

Phil. And lo! Calippus.
Darts with the light'ning's fpeed acrofs the ifle.

G *Evan.*

Evan. Thou at the Senate-house convene my friends;
Melanthon, Dion, and their brave associates,
Will shew that liberty has leaders still.
Anon I'll meet 'em there: my child farewell;
Thou shalt direct me now.

Euph. Too cruel fate!
The tomb is all the mansion I can give;
My mother's tomb!

Phil. You must be brief; th' alarm
Each moment nearer comes. In ev'ry sound
Destruction threatens. Ha! by Heaven this way
Calippus comes—Let me retard his speed. [*Exit.*

EUPHRASIA *coming forward.*

How my distracted heart throbs wild with fear?
What brings Calippus? Wherefore? Save me Heaven!

Enter CALIPPUS.

Calip. This lonely musing in these drear abodes
Alarms suspicion: the king knows thy plottings,
Thy rooted hatred to the state and him.
His sov'reign will commands thee to repair
This moment to his presence.

Euph. Ha! what means
The tyrant?—I obey (*Exit Calippus.*) and, oh! ye Pow'rs,
Ye ministers of Heaven, defend my father;
Support his drooping age; and when anon
Avenging Justice shakes her crimson steel,
Oh! be the grave at least a place of rest;
That from his covert in the hour of peace
Forth he may come to bless a willing people,
And be your own just image here on earth.

END OF THE THIRD ACT.

ACT IV.

Enter MELANTHON *and* PHILOTAS.

Melan. AWAY; no more; pernicious, vile diffembler!
  Phil. Wherefore this frantic rage?
  Melan. Thou can'ft not varnifh
With thy perfidious arts a crime like this.
I climb'd the rugged cliff; but, oh! thou traitor,
Where is Evander? Thro' each dungeon's gloom
I fought the good old king—the guilt is thine;
May vengeance wait thee for it.
  Phil. Still, Melanthon,
Let prudence guide thee.
  Melan. Thou haft plung'd thee down
Far as the loweft depth of hell-born crimes;
Thou haft out-gone all regifters of guilt;
Beyond all fable haft thou finn'd, Philotas.
  Phil. By Heav'n thou wrong'ft me.
Did'ft thou know, old man——
  Melan. Could not his rev'rend age, could not his virtue,
His woes unnumber'd, foften thee to pity?
Thou haft deftroy'd my king.
  Phil. Yet wilt thou hear me?
Your king ftill lives.
  Melan. Thou, vile deceiver!—Lives!
But where?—Away; no more. I charge thee, leave me.
  Phil. We have remov'd him to a place of fafety.
  Melan. Remov'd!--Thou traitor! what dark privacy--
Why move him thence? The dark affaffin's ftab
Has clos'd his days—calm unrelenting villain!
I know it all.

Phil. By ev'ry pow'r above
Evander lives; in safety lives.   Last night
When in his dark embrace sleep wrapt the world,
Euphrasia came, a spectacle of woe;
Dar'd to approach our guard, and with her tears,
With vehemence of grief, she touch'd my heart.
I gave her father to her.
   Melan. How, Philotas!
If thou do'st not deceive me———
   Phil. No, by Heaven!
By ev'ry pow'r above—But hark! those notes
Speak Dionysius near—Anon, my friend,
I'll tell thee each particular;—thy king
Mean while is safe—but lo!- the tyrant comes;
With guilt like his I must equivocate,
And teach ev'n truth and honour to dissemble.

     Enter Dionysius, Calippus, *&c.*

   Dion. Away each vain alarm; the sun goes down,
Nor yet Timoleon issues from his fleet.
There let him linger on the wave-worn beach;
Here the vain Greek shall find another Troy,
A more than Hector here. Tho' Carthage fly,
Ourself—still Dionysius here remains.
And means the Greek to treat of terms of peace?
By Heav'n, this panting bosom hop'd to meet
His boasted phalanx on the embattled plain.
And doth he now, on peaceful councils bent,
Dispatch his herald?—Let the slave approach.

     Enter the Herald.

   Dion. Now speak thy purpose; what doth Greece impart?
   Herald. Timoleon, Sir, whose great renown in arms
Is equall'd only by the softer virtues

Of mild humanity that fway his heart,
Sends me his delegate to offer terms,
On which ev'n foes may well accord; on which
The fierceft nature, tho' it fpurn at juftice,
May fympathize with his.
  Dion. Unfold thy myftery;
Thou fhalt be heard.
  Herald. The gen'rous leader fees,
With pity fees, the wild deftructive havock
Of ruthlefs war; he hath furvey'd around
The heaps of flain that cover yonder field,
And touch'd with gen'rous fenfe of human woe,
Weeps o'er his victories.
  Dion. Your leader weeps!
Then let the author of thofe ills thou fpeak'ft of,
Let the ambitious factor of deftruction,
Timely retreat, and clofe the fcene of blood.
Why doth affrighted peace behold his ftandard
Uprear'd in Sicily? and wherefore here
The iron ranks of war, from which the fhepherd
Retires appall'd, and leaves the blafted hopes
Of half the year, while clofer to her breaft
The mother clafps her infant?
  Herald. 'Tis not mine
To plead Timoleon's caufe; not mine the office
To juftify the ftrong, the righteous motives
That urge him to the war: the only fcope
My deputation aims at, is to fix
An interval of peace, a paufe of horror,
That they, whofe bodies on the naked fhore
Lie weltering in their blood, from either hoft
May meet the laft fad rites to nature due,
And decent lie in honourable graves.
  Dion. Go tell your leader, his pretexts are vain.
Let him, with thofe that live, embark for Greece,

                              And

And leave our peaceful plains; the mangled limbs
Of thofe he murder'd, from my tender care
Shall meet due obfequies.
    Herald. The hero, Sir,
Wages no war with thofe, who bravely die.
'Tis for the dead I fupplicate; for them
We fue for peace; and to the living too
Timoleon would extend it, but the groans
Of a whole people have unfheath'd his fword.
A fingle day will pay the funeral rites.
To morrow's fun may fee both armies meet
Without hoftility, and all in honour;
You to interr the troops, who bravely fell;
We, on our part, to give an humble fod
To thofe, who gain'd a footing on the ifle,
And by their death have conquer'd.
    Dion. Be it fo;
I grant thy fuit: foon as to-morrow's dawn
Illume the world, the rage of wafting war
In vain fhall thirft for blood: but mark my words;
If the next orient fun behold you here,
That hour fhall fee me terrible in arms
Deluge yon plain, and let deftruction loofe.
Thou know'ft my laft refolve, and now farewel.
Some careful officer conduct him forth.   [*Exit Herald.*
By Heav'n the Greek hath offered to my fword
An eafy prey; a facrifice to glut
My great revenge. Calippus let each foldier
This night refign his wearied limbs to reft,
That ere the dawn, with renovated ftrength,
On the unguarded, unfufpecting foe,
Difarm'd, and bent on fuperftitious rites,
From every quarter we may rufh undaunted,
Give the invaders to the deathful fteel,
And by one carnage bury all in ruin.

My

My valiant friends haste to your several posts,
And let this night calm unruffled spirit
Lie hush'd in sleep—Away, my friends, disperse.
Philotas, wait Euphrasia as we order'd?
  Philo. She's here at hand.
  Dion. Admit her to our presence.
Rage and despair, a thousand warring passions,
All rise by turns, and piece-meal rend my heart.
Yet ev'ry means, all measures must be tried,
To sweep the Grecian spoiler from the land,
And fix the crown unshaken on my brow.

Enter EUPHRASIA.

  Euph. What sudden cause requires Euphrasia's presence?
  Dion. Approach, fair mourner, and dispel thy fears.
Thy grief, thy tender duty to thy father,
Has touch'd me nearly. In his lone retreat
Respect, attendance, ev'ry lenient care
To soothe affliction, and extend his life,
Evander has commanded.
  Euph. Vile dissembler!
Detested homicide! (*Aside*)—And has thy heart
Felt for the wretched?
  Dion. Urgencies of state
Abridg'd his liberty; but to his person
All honour hath been paid.
  Euph. The righteous Gods
Have mark'd thy ways, and will in time repay
Just retribution.
  Dion. If to see your father,
If here to meet him in a fond embrace,
Will calm thy breast, and dry those beauteous tears,
A moment more shall bring him to your presence.
  Euph. Ha! lead him hither! Sir, to move him now,
Aged, infirm, worn out with toil and years—

No,

No, let me seek him rather—If soft pity
Has touch'd your heart, oh! send me, send me to him.
  Dion. Controul this wild alarm; with prudent care
Philotas shall conduct him; here I grant
The tender interview.
  Euph. Disaftrous fate!
Ruin impends!—This will difcover all;
I'll perifh firft; provoke his utmoft rage,   *(Afide)*
Tho' much I languifh to behold my father,
Yet now it were not fit—approaching night—
At the firft dawn of day—
  Dion. This night, this very hour,
You both muft meet; the time forbids delay.
Together you may ferve the ftate and me.
Thou fee'ft the havock of wide wafting war;
And more, full well you know, are ftill to bleed.
Thou may'ft prevent their fate.
  Euph. Oh! give the means,
And I will blefs thee for it.
  Dion. From a Greek,
Torments have wrung the truth, Thy hufband, Phocion—
  Euph. Oh! fay, fpeak of my Phocion.
  Dion. He; 'tis he
Hath kindled up this war; with treacherous arts
Inflam'd the ftates of Greece, and now the traitor
Comes with a foreign aid to wreft my crown.
  Euph. And does my Phocion fhare Timoleon's glory?
  Dion. With him invefts our walls, and bids rebellion
Erect her ftandard here.
  Euph. Oh! blefs him Gods!
Where'er my hero treads the paths of war,
Lift on his fide; againft the hoftile javelin
Uprear his mighty buckler; to his fword
Lend the fierce whirlwind's rage, that he may come
With wreaths of triumph, and with conqueft crown'd,
                                           And

And his Euphrasia spring with rapture to him,
Melt in his arms, and a whole nation's voice
Applaud my hero with a love like mine!
  Dion. Ungrateful fair! Has not our sovereign will
On thy descendant's fix'd Sicilia's crown?
Have I not vow'd protection to your boy?
  Euph. From thee the crown! From thee! Euphrasia's
    children
Shall on a nobler basis found their rights,
On their own virtue, and a people's choice.
  Dion. Misguided woman!
  Euph. Ask of thee protection!
The father's valour shall protect his boy.
  Dion. Rush not on sure destruction; ere to late
Accept our proffer'd grace. The terms are these;
Instant send forth a message to your husband;
Bid him draw off his Greeks; unmoor his fleet,
And measure back his way. Full well he knows
You and your father are my hostages;
And for his treason both may answer.
  Euph. Think'st thou then
So meanly of my Phocion?—Dost thou deem him
Poorly wound up to a mere fit of valour,
To melt away in a weak woman's tear?
Oh! thou dost little know him; know'st but little
Of his exalted soul. With gen'rous ardour
Still will he urge the great, the glorious plan,
And gain the ever honour'd bright reward,
Which fame intwines around the patriot's brow,
And bids for ever flourish on his tomb,
For nations free'd and tyrants laid in dust.
  Dion. By Heav'n, this night Evander breathes his last.
  Euph. Better for him to sink at once to rest,
Than linger thus beneath the gripe of famine,
In a vile dungeon scoop'd with barb'rous skill

H   Deep

Deep in the flinty rock; a monument
Of that fell malice and that black fuspicion
That mark'd your father's reign; a dungeon drear
Prepar'd for innocence!—Vice liv'd fecure,
It flourish'd, triumph'd, grateful to his heart;
'Twas virtue only could give umbrage; then,
In that black period, to be great and good
Was a ftate crime; the pow'rs of genius then
Were a conftructive treafon.

 Dion. Ha! beware,
Nor with vile calumny provoke my rage.

 Euph. Whate'er was laudable, whate'er was worthy,
Sunk under foul oppreffion; freeborn men
Were torn in private from their houfehold gods,
Shut from the light of Heaven in cavern'd cells,
Chain'd to the grunfel edge, and left to pine
In bitternefs of foul; while in the vaulted roof
The tyrant fat, and through a fecret channel
Collected ev'ry found; heard each complaint
Of martyr'd virtue; kept a regifter
Of fighs and groans by cruelty extorted;
Noted the honeft language of the heart;
Then on the victim's wreak'd his murd'rous rage,
For yielding to the feelings of their nature.

 Dion. Obdurate woman! obftinate in ill!
Here ends all parley. Now your father's doom
Is fix'd; irrevocably fix'd; this night
Thou fhalt behold him, while inventive cruelty
Purfues his wearied life through every nerve.
I fcorn all dull delay. This very night
Shall fate my great revenge.   [*Exit.*

 Euph. This night perhaps
Shall whelm thee down, no more to blaft creation.
My father, who inhabit'ft with the dead,
Now let me feek thee in the lonely tomb,
And tremble there with anxious hope and fear. [*Exit.*

Scene the Inside of the Temple.

Enter PHOCION *and* MELANTHON.

Pho. Each step I move, a grateful terror shakes
My frame to dissolution.
   Melan. Summon all
Thy wonted firmness; in that dreary vault
A living king is number'd with the dead.
I'll take my post, near where the pillar'd isle
Supports the central dome, that no alarm
Surprize you in the pious act.   [*Exit.*
   Pho. If here
They both are found; if in Evander's arms
Euphrasia meets my search, the fates atone
For all my suff'rings, all afflictions past.
Yes I will seek them—ha!—the gaping tomb
Invites my steps—now be propitious Heaven!
                    [*He enters the Tomb.*

Enter EUPHRASIA.

All hail ye caves of horror!—In this gloom
Divine content can dwell, the heartfelt tear,
Which, as it falls, a father's trembling hand
Will catch, and wipe the sorrows from my eye.
Thou Pow'r supreme! whose all-pervading mind
Guides this great frame of things; who now behold'st me,
Who in that cave of death art full as perfect
As in the gorgeous palace, now, while night
Broods o'er the world, I'll to thy sacred shrine,
And supplicate thy mercies to my father.
Who's there?—Evander?—Answer—quickly say—
                                  Enter

Enter PHOCION *from the Tomb.*

Pho. What voice is that?—Melanthon!—
Euph. Ha! those sounds!—
Speak of Evander; tell me that he lives,
Or lost Euphrasia dies.
Pho. Heart-swelling transport!
Art thou Euphrasia?—'Tis thy Phocion, love;
Thy husband comes.—
Euph. Support me; reach thy hand—
Pho. Once more I clasp her in this fond embrace!
Euph. What miracle has brought thee to me?
Pho. Love
Urg'd me on, and guided all my ways.
Euph. Oh! thou dear wanderer! But wherefore here,
Why in this place of woe?—My tender little one,
Say is he safe?—Oh! satisfy a mother;
Speak of my child, or I go wild at once;
Tell me his fate, and tell me all thy own.
Pho. Your boy is safe, Euphrasia; lives to reign
In Sicily; Timoleon's guardian care
Protects him in his camp; dispel thy fears;
The Gods once more will give him to thy arms.
Euph. My father lives sepulchred ere his time.
Here in Eudocia's tomb; let me conduct thee—
Pho. I came this moment thence—
Euph. And saw Evander?
Pho. Alas! I found him not.
Euph. Not found him there
Have there fell murderers—Oh! [*faints away,*
Pho. I've been too rash; revive, my love, revive;
Thy Phocion calls; the Gods will guard Evander,
And save him to reward thy matchless virtue.

Enter EVANDER *and* MELANTHON.

Evan. Lead me, Melanthon, guide my aged steps;
Where is he? Let me see him.

Pho. My Euphrasia;
Thy father lives;———thou venerable man!
Behold!———I cannot fly to thy embrace.
  Euph. These agonies must end me—Ah! my father!
Again I have him; gracious Pow'rs! again
I clasp his hand, and bathe it with my tears.
  Evan. Euphrasia! Phocion too! Yes, both are here;
Oh! let me thus, thus strain you to my heart.
  Pho. Protected by a daughter's tender care,
By my Euphrasia sav'd! That sweet reflection
Exalts the bliss to rapture.
  Euph. Why my father,
Why thus adventure forth?———The strong alarm
O'erwhelm'd my spirits.
  Evan. I went forth, my child,
When all was dark, and awful silence round,
To throw me prostrate at the altar's foot,
To crave the care of Heaven for thee and thine.
Melanthon there———

Enter PHILOTAS.

  Euph. Philotas!———ha!———what means———
  Phil. Inevitable ruin hovers o'er you:
The tyrant's fury mounts into a blaze;
Unsated yet with blood, he calls aloud
For thee, Evander; thee his rage hath order'd
This moment to his presence.
  Evan. Lead me to him:
His presence hath no terror for Evander.
  Euph. Horror!———It must not be.
  Phil. No; never, never:
I'll perish rather.———But the time demands
Our utmost vigour; with the light'ning's speed
Decisive, rapid.—With the scorpion stings

Of conscience lash'd, despair and horror seize him,
And guilt but serves to goad his tortur'd mind
To blacker crimes. His policy has granted
A day's suspense from arms; yet even now
His troops prepare, in the dead midnight hour,
With base surprise, to storm Timoleon's camp.

Evan. And doth he grant a false insidious truce,
To turn the hour of peace to blood and horror?

Euph. I know the monster well: when specious seeming
Becalms his looks, the rankling heart within
Teems with destruction. Like our own mount Ætna,
When the deep snows invest his hoary head,
And a whole winter gathers on his brow,
Looking tranquility; ev'n then beneath
The fuel'd entrails summon all their rage,
Till the affrighted shepherd round him sees
The sudden ruin, the vulcano's burst,
Mountains hurl'd up in air, and moulten rocks,
And all the land with desolation cover'd.

Melan. Now, Phocion, now, on thee our hope depends.
Fly to Timoleon—I can grant a passport—
Rouze him to vengeance; on the tyrant turn
His own insidious arts, or all is lost.

Pho. Evander thou, and thou, my best Euphrasia,
Both shall attend my flight.

Melan. They must remain;
Th' attempt would hazard all.

Euph. Together here
We will remain, safe in the cave of death;
And wait our freedom from thy conqu'ring arm.

Evan. Oh! would the Gods roll back the stream of time,
And give this arm the sinew that it boasted
At Tauromenium, when its force resistless
Mow'd down the ranks of war; I then might guide
The battle's rage, and, ere Evander die,
Add still another laurel to my brow.

Euph. Enough of laurell'd victory your sword
Hath reap'd in earlier days.
    Evan. And shall my sword,
When the great cause of liberty invites,
Remain inactive, unperforming quite?
Youth, second youth rekindles in my veins!
Tho' worn with age, this arm will know its office;
Will shew that victory has not forgot
Acquaintance with this hand.—And yet—O shame!
It will not be: the momentary blaze
Sinks, and expires——I have surviv'd it all;
Surviv'd my reign, my people and myself.
    Euph. Fly, Phocion, fly; Melanthon will conduct thee.
    Melan. And when th' assault begins, my faithful cohorts
Shall form their ranks around this sacred dome.
    Pho. And my poor captive friends, my brave companions
Taken in battle, wilt thou guard their lives?
    Melan. Trust to my care: no danger shall assail them.
    Pho. By Heav'n, the glorious expectation swells
This panting bosom!—Yes, Euphrasia, yes;
Awhile I leave you to the care of Heaven——
Fell Dionysius tremble; ere the dawn
Timoleon thunders at your gates————The rage,
The pent-up rage of twenty thousand Greeks,
Shall burst at once; and the tumultuous roar
Alarm th' astonish'd world. The brazen gates
Asunder shall be rent; the tow'rs, the ramparts,
Shall yield to Grecian valour; death and rage
Thro' the wide cities round shall wade in gore,
And guilty men awake to gasp their last,
Melanthon, come.
    Evan. Yet, ere thou go'st, young man,
Attend my words: tho' guilt may oft provoke,
As now it does, just vengeance on it's head,

In mercy punish it. The rage of slaughter
Can add no trophy to the victor's triumph;
Bid him not shed unnecessary blood.
Conquest is proud, inexorable, fierce;
It is humanity enobles all;
So thinks Evander, and so tell Timoleon.
  Pho. Farewell; the midnight hour shall give you
      freedom.   [*Exit with Melanthon and Philotas.*
  Euph. Ye guardian Deities, watch all his ways.
  Evan. Come, my Euphrasia, in this interval
Together we will seek the sacred altar,
And thank the God, whose presence fills the dome,
For the best gift his bounty could bestow,
The virtue he has giv'n thee; there we'll pour
Our hearts in praise, in tears of adoration,
For all the wond'rous goodness lavish'd on us.

END of the FOURTH ACT.

ACT V.

Enter DIONYSIUS *and* CALIPPUS.

Dion. ERE the day clos'd, while yet the busy eye
Might view their camp, their stations and their guards,
Their preparations for approaching night,
Did'st thou then mark the motions of the Greeks?

Calip. From the watch-tour I saw them: all things spoke
A foe secure, and discipline relax'd.
Their arms thrown idly by, the soldiers stray'd
To one another's tents; their steeds no more
Stood near at hand caparison'd for war;
And from the lines numbers pour'd out, to see
The spot, where the besieg'd had sallied forth,
And the fierce battle rag'd; to view the slain
That lie in heaps upon the crimson beach.
There the fond brother, the afflicted father,
And the friend, sought some vestige of the face
Of him who dy'd in battle; night came on;
Some slowly gain'd their tents; dispers'd around
Whole parties loiter'd, touch'd with deep regret;
War, and its train of duties, all forgot.

Dion. Their folly gives them to my sword: are all
My orders issued?

Calip. All.

Dion. The troops retir'd
To gain recruited vigour from repose?

I   *Calip.*

Calip. The city round lays hush'd in sleep.
Dion. Anon
Let each brave officer, of chosen valour,
Forsake his couch, and with delib'rate spirit,
Meet at the citadel.— An hour at furthest
Before the dawn, 'tis fix'd to storm their camp;
And whelm their men, their arms, and steeds and tents,
In one prodigious ruin. Haste, Calippus,
Fly to thy post, and bid Euphrasia enter. [*Exit Calippus.*
Evander dies this night: Euphrasia too
Shall be dispos'd of. Curse on Phocion's fraud,
That from my pow'r withdrew their infant boy.
In him the seed of future kings were crush'd,
And the whole hated line at once extinguish'd.

Enter EUPHRASIA.

Dion. Once more approach and hear me; 'tis not now
A time to waste in the vain war of words.
A crisis big with horror is at hand.
I meant to spare the stream of blood, that soon
Shall deluge yonder plains. My fair proposals
Thy haughty spirit has with scorn rejected.
And now, by Heav'n, here; in thy very sight,
Evander breathes his last.
    Euph. The truce you've granted
Suspends the rage of war: mean time send forth
The orators of peace with olive crown'd.
Timoleon, good and just, and ever willing
To conquer rather by persuasive truth,
Than by devouring slaughter, will agree
In friendly parley to assert his rights,
And compromise the war.
    Dion. And must I sue
For terms of peace?—To an invader sue?

Since

Since you, the fiend of Syracuse and Greece,
Since you thus urge me on to desp'rate daring,
Your father first—of him I'll be assur'd—
Your father meets his fate.

Euph. If yet there's wanting
A crime to fill the measure of thy guilt,
Add that black murder to the dreadful list;
With that complete the horrors of thy reign.

Dion. Woman, beware: Philotas is at hand,
And to our presence leads Evander. All
Thy dark complottings, and thy treach'rous arts,
Have prov'd abortive.

Euph. Ha!—What new event?
And is Philotas false?—Has he betray'd him? [*Aside.*

Dion. Evander's doom is seal'd—What ho! Philotas;
Now shalt thou see him die in pangs before thee.

Enter PHILOTAS.

Euph. How my heart sinks within me!

Dion. Where's your pris'ner?

Phil. Evander is no more.

Dion. Ha!—Death has robbed me
Of half my great revenge.

Phil. Worn out with anguish
I saw life ebb apace. With studied art
We gave each cordial drop—Alas! in vain;
He heav'd a sigh; invok'd his daughter's name,
Smil'd and expir'd.

Dion. Bring me his hoary head.

Philo. You'll pardon, Sir, my over-hasty zeal.
I gave the body to the foaming surge
Down the steep rock despis'd.

Dion. Now rave and shriek,
And rend your scatter'd hair.   No more Evander
Shall sway Sicilia's sceptre.

Euph. Mighty Gods!
The harden'd heart, the man elate with pride
View with compassion! To the bad extend
Some portion of your mercy; crimes and blood
Have made their souls a seat of desolation,
Of woe, despair and horror! Turn to them
An eye of pity: whom your bounty form'd
To truth, to goodness, and to gen'rous deeds,
On them no more from your bright stores of bliss
You need dispense: their virtue will support them.

Dion. Now then thou feel'st my vengeance.

Euph. Glory in it;
Exult and triumph.   Thy worst shaft is sped.
Yet still th' unconquer'd mind with scorn can view thee;
With the calm sunshine of the breast beholds
Thy pow'r unequal to subdue the soul,
Which virtue form'd, and which the Gods protect.

Dion. Philotas, bear her hence; she shall not live;
This moment bear her hence; you know the rest;
Go, see our will obey'd; that done, with all
A warrior's speed attend me at the citadel;
There meet the heroes, whom this night I'll lead
To freedom, victory, to glorious havock,
To the destruction of the Grecian name. [*Exit.*

Euph. Accept my thanks, Philotas; generous man!
These tears attest th' emotions of my heart.
But oh! should Greece defer—

Philo. Dispel thy fears;
Phocion will bring relief; or should the tyrant
Assault their camp, he'll meet a marshall'd foe.
Let me conduct thee to the silent tomb.

Euph.

Euph. Ah! there Evander, naked and difarm'd,
Defencelefs quite, may meet fome ruffian ftroke.
  Phil. Lo! here's a weapon; bear this dagger to him.
In the drear monument fhould hoftile fteps
Dare to approach him, they muft enter fingly;
This guards the paffage; man by man they die.
There may'ft thou dwell amidft the wild commotion.
  Euph. Ye pitying Gods, protect my father then!
[*Exeunt.*

Scene the Citadel.

CALIPPUS *and feveral Officers.*

  Firft Officer. What new event thus fummons' us
    together?
  Calip. 'Tis great occafion calls;—Timoleon's ardor
Comes rufhing on; his works rife high in air,
Advance each day, and tow'r above our walls.
One brave exploit may free us——Lo! the king.

Enter DIONYSIUS.

  Dion. Ye brave affociates, who fo oft have fhar'd
Our toil and danger in the field of glory,
My fellow-warriors, what no god could promife,
Fortune hath giv'n us.—In his dark embrace
Lo! fleep envelops the whole Grecian camp.
Againft a foe, the outcafts of their country,
Freebooters roving in purfuit of prey,
Succefs by war, or covert ftratagem
Alike is glorious. Then, my gallant friends,
What need of words? The gen'rous call of freedom,
Your wives, your children, your invaded rights,
All that can fteel the patriot breaft with valour,
Expands

Expands and rouzes in the swelling heart.
Follow th' impulsive ardour; follow me,
Your king, your leader; in the friendly gloom
Of night assault their camp; your country's love,
And fame eternal, shall attend the men
Who march'd through blood and horror, to redeem
From the invader's pow'r, their native land.

Calip. Lead to the onset; Greece shall find we bear
Hearts prodigal of blood, when honour calls;
Resolv'd to conquer or to die in freedom.

Dion. Thus I've resolv'd: when the declining moon
Hath veil'd her orb, our silent march begins.
The order thus:—Calippus, thou lead forth
Iberia's sons with the Numidian bands,
And line the shore.—Perdiccas, be it thine
To march thy cohorts to the mountain's foot,
Where the wood skirts the valley; there make halt
Till brave Amyntor stretch along the vale.
Ourself, with the embodied cavalry
Clad in their mail'd cuirass, will circle round
To where their camp extends its furthest line;
Unnumber'd torches there shall blaze at once,
The signal of the charge; then, oh! my friends,
On every side let the wild uproar loose,
Bid massacre and carnage stalk around,
Unsparing, unrelenting; drench your swords
In hostile blood, and riot in destruction.

Enter an Officer.

Dion. Ha! speak; unfold thy purpose.
Officer. Instant arm;
To arms, my liege; the foe breaks in upon us;
The subterraneous pass is theirs; that way
Their band invades the city sunk in sleep.

Dion.

A TRAGEDY.

Dion. Treason's at work; detested, treach'rous villains!
Is this their promis'd truce? Away, my friends,
Rouze all the war; fly to your sev'ral posts,
And instant bring all Syracuse in arms.
[*Exeunt. Warlike Music.*

Enter MELANTHON.

Calip. Melanthon, now collect your faithful bands,
Melan. Do thou pursue the King; attend his steps:
Timoleon lords it in the captive city.
[*Exit* CALIPPUS.

Enter PHILOTAS.

Melan. Philotas, vengeance has begun its work.
Phil. The Gods have sent relief; dismay, and terror,
And wild amaze, and death in ev'ry shape,
Fill the affrighted city.
Melan. Tyrant, now
Th' inevitable hour of fate is come.
Philotas, round the dome that holds Evander
We will arrange our men; there fix our post,
And guard that spot, till, like some God, Timoleon
Still the wild uproar, and bid slaughter cease. [*Exeunt.*

Scene another Part of the City.

Enter DIONYSIUS.

Why sleep the coward slaves? All things conspire;
The Gods are leagu'd; I see them raze my tow'rs;
My walls and bulwarks fall, and Neptune's trident
From its foundation heaves the solid rock.
Pallas directs the storm; her gorgon shield
Glares

Glares in my view, and from the fleet she calls
Her Greeks enrag'd.—In arms I'll meet 'em all.
What, ho! my guards—Arise, or wake no more.

Enter CALIPPUS.

Calip. This way, my liege; our friends, a valiant band,
Assemble here.
Dion. Give me to meet the Greek.
Our only safety lies in brave despair. [*Exeunt.*

Scene the Inside of the Temple.

A Monument in the Middle.

EUPHRASIA, ERIXENE, *and Female Attendants.*

Euph. Which way, Erixene, which way, my virgins,
Shall we direct our steps? What sacred altar
Clasp on our knees?
Erix. Alas! the horrid tumult
Spreads the destruction wide. On ev'ry side
The victor's shouts, the groans of murder'd wretches,
In wild confusion rise. Once more descend
Eudocia's tomb; there thou may'st find a shelter.
Euph. Anon, Erixene, I mean to visit,
Perhaps for the last time, a mother's urn.
This dagger there, this instrument of death,
Should Fortune prosper the fell tyrant's arms,
This dagger then may free me from his pow'r,
And that drear vault intomb us all in peace.
[*Puts up the dagger.*
Hark!—how the uproar swells! Alas what numbers
In Dionysius' cause shall yield their throats
To the destructive sword!—Aloft I climb'd

The

The temple's vaulted roof; the scene beneath
Is horrible to sight, our domes and palaces
Blaze to the sky; and where the flames forbear,
The Greeks enrag'd brandish the gleaming sword.
From the high roofs, to shun the raging fire,
Wretches precipitate their fall. But oh!
No pause, no mercy; to the edge o'th' sword
They give their bodies; butcher'd, gash'd with wounds
They die in mangl'd heaps, and with their limbs
Cover the sanguine pavement.
 Erix. Hark!
 Euph. The Din
Of arms with clearer sound advances. Ha!
That sudden burst! Again! They rush upon us!
The portal opens———Lo! see there—The soldier
Enters; war invades the sacred fane;
No altar gives a sanctuary now.
       [*Warlike music.*

Enter Dionysius *and* Calippus, *with several soldiers.*

 Dion. Here will I mock their siege; here stand at bay,
And brave 'em to the last.
 Calip. Our weary foes
Desist from the pursuit.
 Dion. Tho' all betray me,
Tho' ev'ry God conspire, I will not yield.
If I must fall, the temple's pond'rous roof,
The mansion of the Gods combin'd against me
Shall first be crush'd, and lie in ruin with me.
Euphrasia here! Detested, treach'rous woman!
For my revenge preserv'd! By Heav'n 'tis well;
Vengeance awaits thy guilt, and this good sword
Thus sends thee to atone the bleeding victims
This night has massacred.
    K.   *Calip.*

Calip. (*Holding Dionysius's arm*) My liege forbear;
Her life preserv'd may plead your cause with Greece,
And mitigate your fate.
  Dion. Presumptuous slave!
My rage is up in arms——By Heav'n she dies.——

Enter EVANDER *from the tomb.*

  Evan. Open, thou cave of death, and give me way.
Horror! forbear! Thou murd'rer hold thy hand!
The Gods behold thee, horrible assassin!
Restrain the blow;—it were a stab to Heav'n;
All nature shudders at it!—Will no friend
Arm in a cause like this a father's hand?
Strike at this bosom rather. Lo! Evander
Prostrate and groveling on the earth before thee;
He begs to die; exhaust the scanty drops
That lag about his heart; but spare my child.
  Dion. Evander!—Do my eyes once more behold him?
May the fiends seize Philotas! Treach'rous slave!
'Tis well thou liv'st; thy death were poor revenge
From any hand but mine.   [*Offers to strike.*
  Euph. No, tyrant, no;   (*Rushing before* EVANDER.
I have provok'd your vengeance; through this bosom
Open a passage; first on me, on me
Exhaust your fury; ev'ry Pow'r above
Commands thee to respect that aged head;
His wither'd frame wants blood to glut thy rage;
Strike here; these veins are full; here's blood enough;
The purple tide will gush to glad thy sight.
  Dion. Amazement blasts and freezes ev'ry pow'r!
They shall not live. Ha! the fierce tide of war
                         (*A flourish of trumpets.*
This way comes rushing on.
                         (*Goes to the top of the stage.*
                                          Euph.

Euph. (*Embracing* EVANDER) Oh! thus, my father,
We'll perish thus together.

Dion. Bar the gates;
Close ev'ry passage, and repel their force.

Evan. And must I see thee bleed?—Oh! for a sword!
Bring, bring me daggers!

Euph. Ha!

Dion. (*Coming down the stage*) Guards seize the slave,
And give him to my rage.

Evan. (*Seiz'd by the guards*) Oh! spare her, spare her.
Inhuman villains!——

Euph. Now one glorious effort! (*Aside.*

Dion. Let me dispatch; thou traitor, thus my arm—

Euph. A daughter's arm, fell monster, strikes the blow.
Yes, first she strikes; an injur'd daughter's arm
Sends thee devoted to th' infernal gods. (*Stabs him.*)

Dion. Detested fiend!—Thus by a woman's hand?—
(*He falls.*)

Euph. Yes, tyrant, yes; in a dear father's cause,
A woman's vengeance tow'rs above her sex.

Dion. May curses blast thy arm! May Ætna's fires
Convulse the land; to its foundation shake
The groaning isle! May civil discord bear
Her flaming brand through all the realms of Greece;
And the whole race expire in pangs like mine. (*Dies.*)

Euph. Behold, all Sicily behold!—The point
Glows with the tyrant's blood. Ye slaves, (*to the guards*)
    look there;
Kneel to your rightful king: the blow for freedom
Gives you the rights of men!—And oh! my father,
My ever honour'd sire, it gives thee life.

Evan. My child; my daughter; sav'd again by thee!
(*He embraces her.*

A flourish of trumpets.

Enter PHOCION, MELANTHON, PHILOTAS, &c.

Pho. Now let the monster yield.—My best Euphrasia!
Euph. My lord! my Phocion! welcome to my heart.
Lo! there the wonders of Euphrasia's arm!
  Pho. And is the proud one fall'n! The dawn shall see him
A spectacle for public view.——Euphrasia!
Evander too!—Thus to behold you both——
  Evan. To her direct thy looks; there fix thy praise,
And gaze with wonder there. The life I gave her—
Oh! she has us'd it for the noblest ends!
To fill each duty; make her father feel
The purest joy, the heart-dissolving bliss
To have a grateful child.——But has the rage
Of slaughter ceas'd?
  Pho. It has.
  Evan. Where is Timoleon?
  Pho. He guards the citadel; there gives his orders
To calm the uproar, and recall from carnage
His conqu'ring troops.
  Euph. Oh! once again, my father,
Thy sway shall bless the land. Nor for himself
Timoleon conquers;—to redress the wrongs
Of bleeding Sicily the hero comes.
Thee, good Melanthon, thee, thou gen'rous man,
His justice shall reward.—Thee too, Philotas,
Whose sympathizing heart could feel the touch
Of soft humanity, the hero's bounty,
His brightest honours, shall be lavish'd on thee.
Evander too will place you near his throne;
And shew mankind, ev'n on this shore of being,
That virtue still shall meet its sure reward.
                                              Phil.

A TRAGEDY.

Phil. I am rewarded: feelings such as mine
Are worth all dignities; my heart repays me.
    Evan. Come, let us seek Timoleon; to his care
I will commend ye both: for now, alas!
Thrones and dominions now no more for me.
To her I give my crown. Yes, thou, Euphrasia,
Shalt reign in Sicily.———And oh! ye Pow'rs,
In that bright eminence of care and peril,
Watch over all her ways; conduct and guide
The goodness you inspir'd, that she may prove,
If e'er distress like mine invade the land,
A parent to her people; stretch the ray
Of filial piety to times unborn,
That men may hear her unexampled virtue,
And learn to emulate THE GRECIAN DAUGHTER!

THE END.

POSTSCRIPT.

THE Tragedy, here offered to the Public, is founded on a passage in VALERIUS MAXIMUS *. We are told by that author, "That a woman of ingenuous birth was "convicted before the PRÆTOR of a capital crime, and "delivered over to the TRIUMVIR to be put to death in "prison. The jailer received her into his custody, but, "touched with compassion, did not proceed immediately "to execute the sentence. His humanity went so far as to "admit the daughter of the unhappy criminal into the "gaol; but not without a previous search, lest any "nourishment should be secretly conveyed. To starve "the prisoner to death was his design. Several days "passed, when it became matter of wonder how the poor "woman subsisted so long. The jailer's curiosity was "excited: he watched the daughter narrowly, and saw "her give her breast to the famished mother, and with "her milk supply the cravings of nature. Touched by "the novelty of so affecting a sight, he made his report to "the TRIUMVIR, from whom it reached the PRÆTOR, "and, the whole matter being referred to the JUDICIAL "MAGISTRATES, the mother received a free pardon. "What will not filial piety undertake?—What place "will it not penetrate?—What will it not devise, when "in a dungeon it finds unheard of means to preserve a "parent's life?—Is there, in the course of human affairs, "a scene so big with wonder, as a mother nourished at "the daughter's breast?—The incident might, at the first "view, be thought repugnant to the order of nature, if "TO LOVE OUR PARENTS were not the FIRST LAW "stamped by the hand of Nature on the human heart." Thus far VALERIUS MAXIMUS: He goes on in the same place, and tells a Greek tale, in which the heroine performs the same act of piety to a father in the decline of life. For the purposes of the drama, the latter story has been preferred. The painters long since seized the subject; and by them it has been called ROMAN CHARITY.

The

* Vide Valer. Max. lib. 5, c. 4, de Pietate in Parentes, 7.

POSTSCRIPT.

The Author has taken the liberty to place it in the reign of DIONYSIUS the Younger, at the point of time when TIMOLEON laid siege to SYRACUSE. The general effect, it was thought, would be better produced, if the whole had an air of real history.

Atque ita mentitur, sic veris falsa remiscet,
Primo ne medium, medio ne discrepet imum.

The Author does not wish to conceal that the subject of this Tragedy has been touched in some foreign pieces: but he thinks it has been *only* touched. The ZELMIRE of Monf. BELLOY begins after the daughter has delivered her father out of prison. The play indeed has many beauties; and if the sentiments and business of that piece coincided with the design of THE GRECIAN DAUGHTER, the Author would not have blushed to walk in the same tract. But a new fable was absolutely necessary: and perhaps in the present humour of the times, it is not unlucky that no more than three lines could be adopted from Monf. BELLOY. Every writer, who makes up a story with characters and incidents already hackneyed on the English stage, and invents nothing, cries out with an air of triumph, That he has not borrowed from the wits of FRANCE. In the Isle of Man, it is said, there is an epitaph in these words: " *He who lies here interred, was never* " *out of this island.*" The poor man was to be pitied: a similar inscription upon the tomb stone of a modern poet, would, perhaps, do as little honour to the memory of the deceased.

The Author cannot dismiss his Play, without declaring that, though in love with the subject, he has not satisfied even his own ideas of the drama: he laments that he had neither time nor ability to make it better. To heighten it with additional beauties was reserved for the decorations with which the zeal of Mr. GARRICK has embellished the representation; for the admirable performance of Mr. BARRY; and, above all, for the enchanting powers and the genius of Mrs. BARRY.

www.ingramcontent.com/pod-product-compliance
Lightning Source LLC
Chambersburg PA
CBHW032001230426
43672CB00010B/2234